W9-ATO-837

How to Use This Book

Look for these special features in this book:

SIDEBARS, **CHARTS**, **GRAPHS**, and original **MAPS** expand your understanding of what's being discussed—and also make useful sources for classroom reports.

FAQs answer common **F**requently **A**sked **Q**uestions about people, places, and things.

WOW FACTORS offer "Who knew?" facts to keep you thinking.

TRAVEL GUIDE gives you tips on exploring the state—either in person or right from your chair!

PROJECT ROOM provides fun ideas for school assignments and incredible research projects. Plus, there's a guide to primary sources—what they are and how to cite them.

Please note: All statistics are as up-to-date as possible at the time of publication.

Consultants: Ellen Morris Bishop, Executive Director, Oregon Paleo Lands Institute; David Peterson del Mar, Author and Professor, Portland State University and Oregon State University; William Loren Katz

Book production by The Design Lab

Library of Congress Cataloging-in-Publication Data
Kent, Deborah.
 Oregon / by Deborah Kent.
   p. cm.—(America the beautiful. Third series)
 Includes bibliographical references and index.
 ISBN-13: 978-0-531-18587-2
 ISBN-10: 0-531-18587-7
 1. Oregon—Juvenile literature. I. Title. II. Series.
 F876.3.K36 2008
 979.5—dc22   2007038691

AMERICA ★ THE ★ BEAUTIFUL

Oregon

BY DEBORAH KENT

Third Series

Children's Press®
An Imprint of Scholastic Inc.
New York ★ Toronto ★ London ★ Auckland ★ Sydney
Mexico City ★ New Delhi ★ Hong Kong
Danbury, Connecticut

CONTENTS

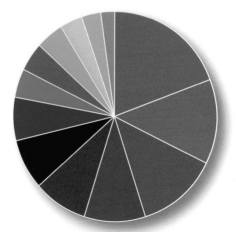

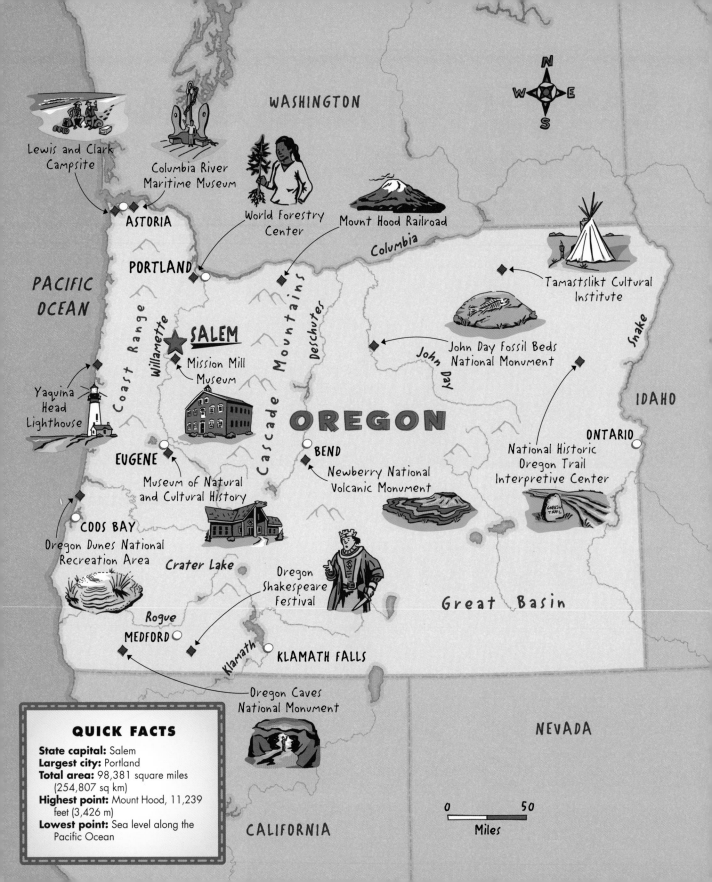

WASHINGTON

Lewis and Clark Campsite

Columbia River Maritime Museum

ASTORIA

World Forestry Center

Mount Hood Railroad

Columbia

PORTLAND

PACIFIC OCEAN

Tamastslikt Cultural Institute

John Day Fossil Beds National Monument

Deschutes

Cascade Mountains

John Day

Snake

SALEM

Mission Mill Museum

Willamette

Coast Range

Yaquina Head Lighthouse

OREGON

ONTARIO

IDAHO

National Historic Oregon Trail Interpretive Center

EUGENE

Museum of Natural and Cultural History

BEND

Newberry National Volcanic Monument

COOS BAY

Oregon Dunes National Recreation Area

Crater Lake

Oregon Shakespeare Festival

Great Basin

Rogue

MEDFORD

Klamath

KLAMATH FALLS

Oregon Caves National Monument

NEVADA

CALIFORNIA

QUICK FACTS

State capital: Salem
Largest city: Portland
Total area: 98,381 square miles (254,807 sq km)
Highest point: Mount Hood, 11,239 feet (3,426 m)
Lowest point: Sea level along the Pacific Ocean

N
W   E
S

0   50
Miles

Welcome to Oregon!

HOW DID OREGON GET ITS NAME?

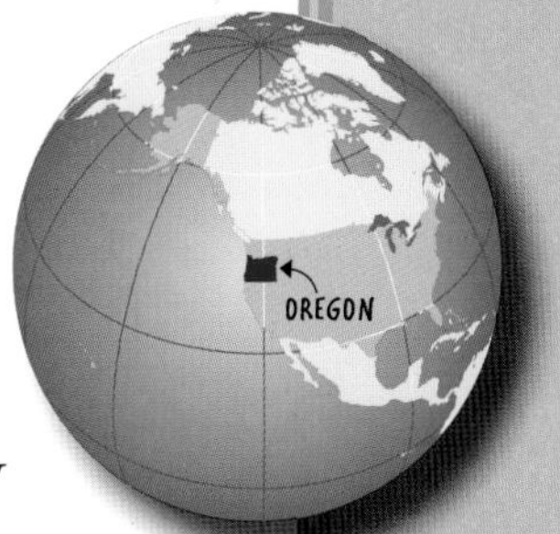

The origin of the name *Oregon* is a long-standing mystery. In 1765, a British army major learned from Native Americans near the Great Lakes about a mighty Ouragon River west of the Rocky Mountains. Early French traders who ran into fierce storms may have named the region after their word for "hurricane," *ouragan*. Spanish explorers may have called the land around the Columbia River's mouth "Aragon," after a province in Spain. It's fitting that a mix of people can claim credit for Oregon's name, given that it took all of them, and more, to make the state what it is today.

OREGON

IDAHO

WYOMING

COLORADO

UTAH

8

READ ABOUT

A view of Mount
Hood and
Trillium Lake

CHAPTER ONE

LAND

★

IF YOU VISIT OREGON, YOU WILL OFTEN FIND YOURSELF LOOKING UP. Or down. Oregon's mountain peaks vanish among the clouds, and its gorges plunge into the distance. Mount Hood, the highest peak in the state, stands 11,239 feet (3,426 meters) above sea level. At Oregon's eastern border with Idaho, Hells Canyon marks the deepest gorge in North America—nearly 8,000 feet (2,400 m) deep! In southern Oregon, Crater Lake, at 1,996 feet (608 m) deep, is the deepest lake in the United States.

Oregon Topography

Use the color-coded elevation chart to see on the map Oregon's high points (dark red to orange) and low points (green). Elevation is measured as the distance above or below sea level.

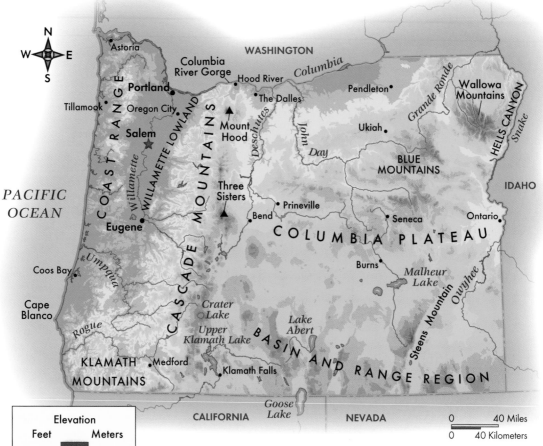

GETTING TO KNOW OREGON

Oregon lies along the Pacific coast in the northwestern region of the United States. The Columbia River divides most of it from the state of Washington, its neighbor to the north. Idaho lies to the east, and California and Nevada to the south. Oregon is roughly rectangular in

Oregon Geo-Facts

Along with the state's geographical highlights, this chart ranks Oregon's land, water, and total area compared to all other states.

Total area; rank . . . . .98,381 square miles (254,807 sq km); 9th
Land; rank . . . . .95,997 square miles (248,632 sq km); 10th
Water; rank . . . . .2,384 square miles (6,175 sq km); 19th
Inland water; rank . . . . .1,050 square miles (2,719 sq km); 19th
Coastal water; rank . . . . .80 square miles (207 sq km); 17th
Territorial water; rank . . . . . . .1,254 square miles (3,248 sq km); 9th
Geographic center . . . .Crook, 25 miles (40 km) south-southeast of Prineville
Latitude . . . . .42° N to 46°15′ N
Longitude . . . . 116°45′ W to 124°30′ W
Highest point . . . . Mount Hood, 11,239 feet (3,426 m)
Lowest point . . . . Sea level along the Pacific Ocean
Largest city . . . . .Portland

Source: U.S. Census Bureau

Oregon is 296 miles (476 kilometers) long from north to south along its western border. But when you add up all the islands, points, and inlets, the state actually has 1,410 miles (2,269 km) of shoreline!

shape. Its southern border is almost ruler-straight. The northern edge curves gently with the natural bends of the Columbia, and the Snake River forms part of the border with Idaho. The Pacific coast is jagged with bays, inlets, and rocky islands.

MOLDING THE LAND

The earth's crust is made up of giant plates that fit together roughly like the pieces of a jigsaw puzzle. Slowly and relentlessly, these plates move from place to place. More than 100 million years ago, Oregon's first land was formed. It lay on the western rim of the North American plate.

A couple canoes on Sparks Lake near Broken Top Mountain in the Cascade Range.

As this plate pushed westward, it collided with other plates and islands off its coast. The islands it nudged up against had been formed by undersea volcanoes. These islands became mountains on the mainland as Oregon grew. As the North American plate, with its newly added Oregon land, continued to move westward, it pushed over the Pacific seafloor. Deep beneath the surface, rock began to melt. The melted rock rose toward the surface, creating volcanoes, including the Cascade Range, which is still active today.

LAND REGIONS

Oregon's mountains and valleys divide the state into several distinct areas. Oregon has seven land regions: the Coast Range Region, the Willamette Lowland, the Cascade Mountains, the Klamath Mountains, the Columbia **Plateau**, the Blue Mountains and Hells Canyon, and the Basin and Range Region.

WORD TO KNOW

plateau *an elevated part of the earth with steep slopes*

Coast Range Region

Along the Oregon coast, pounding waves have carved spectacular cliffs. Although parts of Oregon's coast are rocky and rugged, the state also has many beautiful beaches. In some places, the wind has gathered beach sand into great hills called dunes. Natural rock sculptures called sea stacks tower offshore.

Along Oregon's Pacific coast are a series of low, rolling mountain ranges. The Coast Ranges, as they are called, are the lowest mountains in the state. They average about 2,000 feet (610 m) in height. In many spots, sheer cliffs rise from the sea. In other places, the mountains are like a series of steps.

Willamette Lowland

Between the Coast Range Region and the Cascades lies the fertile Willamette Lowland. The Willamette River and its branches drain most of the lowland. The Willamette River is a major **tributary** of the Columbia, North America's fourth-largest river.

With its heavy flow and steep drop, the Columbia River generates more **hydroelectric power** than any river in North America.

WORDS TO KNOW

tributary *a river that flows into a larger river*

hydroelectric power *electricity generated by the force of water passing over a dam*

A photographer captures the scenery of Cape Kiwanda along the Oregon coast.

Cascade Mountains

The beautiful Cascade Mountains run like a spine down Oregon from north to south. The state's loftiest peaks rise in this range. Mount Hood towers 11,239 feet (3,426 m) above sea level. Hot springs gurgle near the summit of this active volcano. Mount Jefferson rises 10,497 feet (3,199 m). The Three Sisters are a cluster of peaks, each more than 10,000 feet (3,000 m) tall. The catastrophic eruption of an ancient volcano called Mount Mazama formed Crater Lake in the southern Cascades. The lake and the surrounding scenic area are preserved within Crater Lake National Park.

Klamath Mountains

More rugged peaks stand in the Klamath Mountains, which span southwestern Oregon and northwestern California. These mountains include some of Oregon's oldest rocks. Oregon's highest peak in this range is Mount Ashland, at 7,533 feet (2,296 m). In the north, the Klamaths are called the Siskiyou Mountains. Many parts of this region are preserved as wilderness areas.

Crater Lake is the seventh-deepest lake in the world!

Hikers along the edge of Crater Lake

The Snake River runs through Hells Canyon.

The Columbia Plateau

This high, dry rugged plateau spreads east of the Cascades. The John Day and Deschutes rivers, which form deep scenic gorges, cut through the plateau.

The Blue Mountains and Hells Canyon

Oregon's oldest rocks and deepest gorge are found in its northeastern corner. **Glaciers** carved the region's Wallowa and Elkhorn mountains, which reach almost 10,000 feet (3,000 m) high. Hells Canyon, which lies on the border between Oregon and Idaho, is the deepest river gorge in North America. From the rim on the Oregon side, you can see the Snake River flowing more than a mile below you. The canyon is 10 miles (16 km) wide at its broadest point.

The Basin and Range Region

Oregon's southeastern corner lies within the Basin and Range Region. This region extends south into Nevada. It is a dry area of steep-sided mountains and bowl-shaped valleys called basins. Steens Mountain rises high above the surrounding desert land.

WORD TO KNOW

glaciers *slow-moving masses of ice*

Weather Report

TEMPERATURE
119°F

TEMPERATURE
-54°F

This chart shows record temperatures (high and low) for the state, as well as average temperatures (July and January) and average annual precipitation.

Record high temperature . . . . 119°F (48°C)
    at Prineville on July 29, 1898, and at Pendleton on August 10, 1898
Record low temperature . . . . −54°F (−48°C)
    at Ukiah on February 9, 1933, and at Seneca on February 10, 1933
Average July temperature . . . . 68°F (20°C)
Average January temperature . . . . 40°F (4°C)
Average annual precipitation . . . . .37 inches (94 cm)

Source: National Climatic Data Center, NESDIS, NOAA, U.S. Department of Commerce

Portland is one of the cloudiest cities in the United States. In an average year, the sun breaks through only 39 percent of the time during daylight hours!

ROUGH WEATHER!

Although the climate in Oregon is generally mild, fierce windstorms and unusually heavy rains sometimes pound the state. On Columbus Day, October 12, 1962, a windstorm battered the Oregon coast and caused major damage as far east as the Willamette Valley. It destroyed homes and barns and uprooted thousands of trees. Heavy rains in January and February 1996 caused many streams and rivers in western Oregon to overflow their banks, resulting in major flood damage in Oregon City and Tillamook. Ten years later, on December 14–15, 2006, a Pacific storm with high winds and heavy rain struck Oregon and Washington. Some 350,000 people in Oregon lost power, and eight people were reported dead or missing.

CLIMATE

When it comes to weather, Oregon is all over the map. That is to say, the state's climate differs widely from one region to another. Oregon has sun-parched expanses, snow-capped mountains, and some of the rainiest spots in the country.

Warm, moist breezes from the Pacific fan the coast of Oregon. Places west of the Cascades tend to have a mild climate and receive generous rainfall. Some places on the west slopes of the Coast Ranges get up to 200 inches (508 centimeters) of rain each year.

The mighty Cascades form a barrier, blocking rain-laden winds from reaching the eastern part of the state. When you travel east over the mountains, you see a dramatic change. Within a few minutes, you pass from the green, forested western slopes to the open grasslands on the eastern side. While western Oregon is wet, especially in the winter, portions of the eastern two-thirds of the state may receive as little as 15 inches (38 cm) of rain a year. The driest parts of Oregon are in the Columbia Plateau and the Basin and Range.

Oregon National Park Areas

This map shows some of Oregon's national parks, monuments, preserves, and other areas protected by the National Park Service.

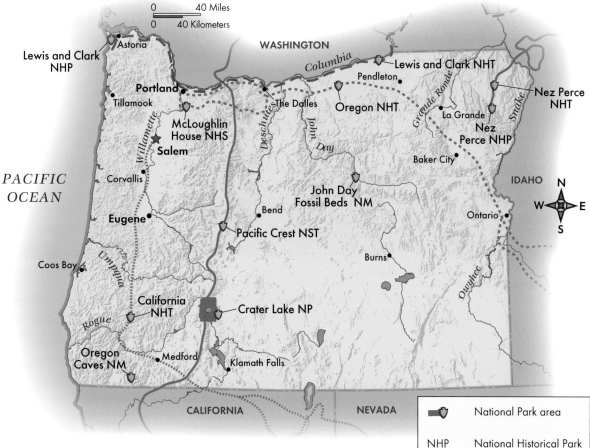

![National Park area symbol]	National Park area
NHP	National Historical Park
NHS	National Historic Site
NHT	National Historic Trail
NM	National Monument
NP	National Park

PLANT LIFE

The varieties of plant life in Oregon reflect the differences in the state's climate. Thick forests flourish from the coast to the western slopes of the Cascades. Pines and redwoods tower more than 100 feet (30 m) above the ground. Cedars, spruces, hemlocks, willows, and cottonwoods grow on hillsides and along streams. The dominant tree in western Oregon is the Douglas fir.

Many elk make their home in Oregon forests.

Marmot

Several kinds of sagebrush grow in arid eastern Oregon. Though it is dry, this part of the state supports some tall trees, especially the stately ponderosa pine.

Many species of wildflowers bloom in Oregon. Among them are buttercups, Indian pipes, and Oregon grapes, Oregon's state flower.

ANIMAL LIFE

Oregon's forests shelter many fur-bearing mammals, including foxes, coyotes, bobcats, and raccoons. Beavers change the landscape by damming streams to create ponds. The call of the marmot (a rodent similar to a woodchuck) is heard in the high Cascades. In the 1800s, hunting killed off several animal species in eastern Oregon that have since been reintroduced, including elk, mountain goats, and bighorn sheep.

ENDANGERED SPECIES

Oregon has 37 animal species listed as threatened or endangered, including the Oregon silverspot butterfly, the northern spotted owl, the Lahontan cutthroat trout, and several kinds of salmon. Fourteen Oregon plant species are listed as threatened or endangered, including the marsh sandwort, the golden paintbrush, the Willamette daisy, Kincaid's lupine, and McFarlane's four-o'clock.

Northern spotted owl

Black bears and cougars prowl the mountains. Mule deer, black-tailed deer, and elk graze in mountain meadows. Pronghorns can sometimes be seen dashing over the high plateau. Whales and porpoises cavort along the coast. Playful sea otters swim near the mouths of Oregon's coastal rivers.

Oregon's streams are home to many different fish, including perch, bass, and steelhead trout. Salmon spend most of their lives in the ocean but battle their way upstream to lay eggs. The journey of thousands of salmon, fighting the fierce currents of the Columbia and other Oregon rivers, is one of nature's wonders.

In the spring, forests and grasslands ring with birdsong. The flute-voiced western meadowlark is Oregon's state bird. Other songbirds include the hermit thrush, the wood peewee, and the western bluebird. The bald eagle and the golden eagle are breathtaking sights as they circle in search of prey.

MINI-BIO

OPAL WHITELEY: A CHILD OF NATURE

As a child, Opal Whiteley (1897–1992) loved the birds and animals near her home in Walden. As a teenager, she began to teach classes about the natural world to children and adults around the state. A 1920 best seller called *The Story of Opal: The Journal of an Understanding Heart* claimed to be based on a diary Whiteley began at the age of six. With her deep love of nature, she became an important symbol for many who sought to preserve Oregon's natural beauty. Her life has inspired several books and even a Broadway musical titled *Opal*.

? Want to know more?
See www.efn.org/~opal/

THINK ABOUT IT!

Saving Old-Growth Forests

During the late 1980s and early 1990s, the northern spotted owl, a little-known bird of the Northwest, became the subject of a fierce controversy. The northern spotted owl lives in old-growth forest—that is, forest that has never been cut for timber. A wide variety of trees and smaller plants grow in old-growth forest, which makes it a unique natural environment. The northern spotted owl is one of several species that require this environment in order to survive. Its presence is considered an indicator of the health and stability of the entire environment. In the early decades of the 20th century, vast tracts of Oregon's old-growth forest fell to the logger's ax. By 1990, only a small percentage of the state's original forest remained intact.

If the last old-growth forests are logged, the northern spotted owl will almost surely become extinct. According to federal law, industry cannot destroy the habitat of an endangered species. Environmentalists saw the plight of the northern spotted owl as a way to save the last old-growth forests in Oregon. They filed lawsuits to stop future logging in the owl's habitat.

Thousands of people in rural Oregon depend on logging for their livelihood. Loggers and their families were angry and frightened by efforts to halt the cutting of old-growth timber. Bumper stickers proclaimed, "JOBS, NOT OWLS!" At a public hearing in Lebanon, after some logging was stopped, a tearful woman declared, "My husband took a $12,000 drop in wages. How am I going to feed my child?"

As a result of the lawsuits, logging in the old-growth forests dropped sharply. Many loggers had to change jobs. But as Jerry Franklin, a scientist at the University of Washington, points out, "There is no hope for the spotted owl without habitat." Scientists continue to work to try to save the spotted owl and the magnificent forests in which it and many species live.

A salmon ladder at the Bonneville Dam on the Columbia River

CARING FOR THE LAND

Many laws in Oregon protect the state's air, water, and other resources. The state was at the forefront of the movement to require deposits on beverage containers as a way to encourage people to recycle them, which, in turn, helps cut down on roadside litter. Most of Oregon's beaches and coastal bluffs are preserved as public parkland, unlike waterfront property in many states. Salmon ladders help salmon swim over dams on their upstream journey to lay their eggs, and in some streams, dams are being removed to help fish and wildlife. Concerned Oregonians value the environment and want to preserve it for future generations.

READ ABOUT

Prehistoric people
used spears
to hunt large
game animals.

c. 16,000 BCE
*People first enter what is
now Oregon*

2500 BCE ▲
*People on the Columbia
River learn to dry and
store salmon*

c. 1000 BCE
*People learn to hunt with
bows and arrows*

CHAPTER TWO

FIRST PEOPLE

★

PEOPLE FIRST ENTERED NORTH AMERICA FROM ASIA WHEN GREAT GLACIERS CONNECTED THE TWO CONTINENTS. These hunters followed herds of mammoths and other large game animals. Gradually, the ice sheet melted, the sea level rose, and water separated Asia from North America. People first arrived in what is now Oregon in about 16,000 BCE.

500 CE

A trading center develops at the site of The Dalles

1720s ▶

Horses reach the Columbia Plateau

1790

About 22,000 Native people live on Oregon's coast

Archaeologists found a collection of sagebrush sandals in an Oregon cave that are thought to be 10,000 years old.

WORDS TO KNOW

archaeologists *people who study the remains of past human societies*

pemmican *dried salmon or other meat*

Digging stick from the Columbia Plateau

EARLY PEOPLES

Oregon's first people hunted with spears and fished with hooks made of bone. They lived in small family groups, moving from place to place as they followed the herds. For the people along Oregon's rivers and streams, life revolved around the yearly migration of the salmon. As great schools of salmon headed upstream to lay their eggs, people waited along the banks with nets and spears. But food was plentiful only while the salmon run lasted. There was no way to preserve extra fish for leaner times.

Sometime around 2500 BCE, people near the present-day city of The Dalles discovered they could dry salmon on wooden racks in the sun. Carefully dried salmon, or **pemmican**, became a valuable food. Pemmican could be stored for months or even years at a time. It was rich in protein and vitamins. Eventually, this food was in great demand by people who lived farther inland. By around 500 CE, The Dalles became a lively trading center. People from all over the Northwest traveled there to trade for pemmican and other goods.

Forests were filled with deer, elk, and bears. About 1000 BCE, hunters developed bows and arrows. These were good weapons to use when hunting small game, because the arrows could be fired with great accuracy.

Ways of life varied greatly among Oregon's early people. Along the coast and lower end of the Columbia River, people settled in villages. A powerful chief headed each village, and some families were wealthier than others. On the Columbia Plateau and in the Great Basin, people lived in small groups that were always on the move. In general, people within these bands had equal standing with one another. The hardships of day-to-day life kept anyone from gathering much wealth.

Native American Peoples
(Before European Contact)
This map shows the general area of Native American peoples before European settlers arrived.

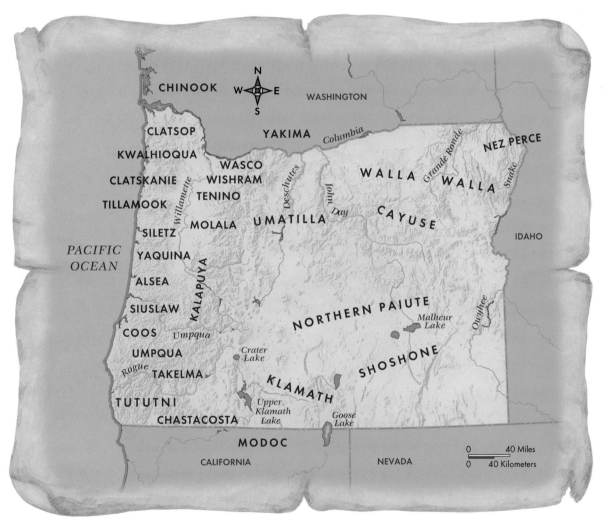

By the late 1700s, about two dozen languages were spoken in what is now Oregon. There may have been as many as 50 distinct groups. These people fall roughly into three groups: the people of the Columbia Plateau, the Basin and Range, and the coast.

Nez Perce women and their mat-covered dwellings, called longhouses

PEOPLE OF THE COLUMBIA PLATEAU

Forests and streams provided food for the people of the Columbia Plateau. They harvested salmon and other fish, and hunted elk, deer, and smaller game. In order to create grazing areas for game, they set fire to the forest undergrowth. This practice created open grass-lands and forests of fire-resistant trees such as oak and ponderosa pine.

Many nations lived in the Columbia Plateau, including Umatillas, Nez Perces, Cayuses, and Klamaths. For part of the year, they lived in villages. At other times, they packed up their belongings and moved to hunting grounds. Everyone worked hard for the group's survival, and everyone's efforts were valued. Although each group had a chief or headman (or occasionally a headwoman), there was no royalty.

PEOPLE OF THE BASIN AND RANGE

Northern Paiutes lived in Oregon's Basin and Range Region, the most barren part of the state. An unending search for food shaped their lives. People hunted small game such as rabbits and birds, and killed deer when they could find them. Women and children gathered seeds, roots, and berries. They also caught crickets and grasshoppers, a rich source of protein that they ate raw or fried.

A Paiute water basket

Northern Paiutes never stayed in one place for very long. They moved every few months, always heading toward a new food supply. In the spring, they went to places where they could collect edible seeds and roots. In summer, they spread out to gather and dry crickets, berries, and more seeds. In summer and fall, the women gathered pine nuts to last through the winter, while the men hunted game. In the winter, when game and other food were hard to find, the people lived in tiny huts made of willow branches. They lived on the food they had stored and waited for spring to come again.

Scientists estimate that on average, the Native Americans along the Oregon coast ate 365 pounds (166 kilograms) of salmon per person per year, or 1 pound (0.45 kg) of salmon a day!

Q8 HOW DID THE COASTAL PEOPLE CATCH SALMON?

A8 Most salmon fishing was done with large nets, or seines. One seine could be 16 feet (5 m) wide and as much as 600 feet (180 m) long! Heavy stones held down one end and wooden floats kept the other end on the water's surface. The net formed a standing wall in the water. Any fish that swam into it were trapped.

WORD TO KNOW

symmetry *balance, evenness on both sides*

PEOPLE OF THE COAST

Historians believe about 22,000 Native Americans lived along the coast of Oregon by 1790. Among the nations were the Chinook, the Clatsop, and the Tillamook.

The coastal peoples lived in a land of abundance. The ocean and rivers gave them all the fish and shellfish they could eat. Because they rarely had to worry about finding food, the coastal people had time to develop arts such as dance, carving, canoe building, and story-telling. The Wasco people, who lived along the Lower Columbia River, shared many characteristics of the coastal cultures because they too had an abundant food source—salmon.

The coastal people generally lived in towns or villages, in houses built of cedar planks, supported by a framework of poles. Some houses were as long as 100 feet (30 m) and sheltered several families. Sleeping platforms stood on posts about 5 feet (1.5 m) above the ground. Families stored food, clothing, pottery, and other things in the space underneath.

Clatsops, Chinooks, and other coastal peoples traveled up and down the rivers and along the coast in canoes made from hollowed-out logs. One early white visitor wrote with admiration, "Their canoes are made of cedar, and although [they] possess no other instrument than a small chisel, it would be in vain for any white (with every tool he could wish) to set up a competition with them in this art; if perfect **symmetry**, smoothness, and proportion constitute beauty, they surpass anything I ever beheld."

As time passed, some people in the coastal towns gathered more wealth and power than others. Eventually, the people of these groups fell into three social classes. The chiefs and their extended families

Salmon fishing in the Columbia River

formed the richest and most powerful class. Custom allowed a chief to have several wives. They were considered to be his possessions. The chief's first wife was the most important, and she directed the wives who came later.

The largest class consisted of commoners, who fished, hunted, and made canoes. Beneath the commoners were slaves, mostly people who had been captured in warfare with other nations. Few in number, enslaved people were largely seen as symbols of wealth

WORDS TO KNOW

breechcloths *garments worn by men over their lower bodies*

obsidian *jet-black volcanic glass*

This painting shows a Chinook woman holding her baby in a head-flattening board.

for their owners and weren't heavily relied on for their labor. Sometimes, enslaved people were used as trade goods. Traded from one people to another, slaves might travel hundreds of miles from their original home.

DRESS AND ADORNMENT

Coastal women wore skirts made of animal skins or woven from strips of cedar bark. The skirt hung from the woman's waist by a leather belt and reached below her knees. Men wore skin **breechcloths** wrapped around the waist and thighs. Both men and women pierced their noses. Some jewelry was made from **obsidian** and other stones that came from as far away as Mexico.

Soon after a baby was born into a chief's family, the mother strapped a pair of boards to the baby's forehead. Pressing on both the top and bottom of the child's head, the boards gradually flattened the soft bone of the child's skull. A flattened head was considered a mark of nobility. Only slaves and commoners had ordinary round heads.

ARTS AND LEISURE

Coastal Native Americans carved figures of humans and animals out of wood and bone. They also carved designs of birds, animals, and plants on the posts of their houses and the handles of knives and chisels. Sometimes even the sides of canoes were decorated with carvings.

Dancing was a favorite entertainment of the coastal people. Women and men each danced in their own group. Dances could be graceful and solemn or wild and exciting. A drummer or flute player made music for the dancers to follow.

The coastal people loved to play games of chance. In one game, someone tossed a wooden disk that had carvings on each side. People made bets over which side would show when the disk landed. Sometimes, the stakes got higher and higher as the game went on. Players would lose canoes, houses, and slaves in the betting. Men could even lose their wives!

Storytelling was a favorite pastime in the evenings or at special feast times. Some stories told of disasters that had befallen the group, such as floods or fires. Some described the deeds of great hunters or warriors. Other stories were based on the people's beliefs about the creation of the world. These stories described how the earth was made, how the sun came to be in the sky, and why the fish and forest animals behaved as they did. These stories reflect the close connection between Oregon's first people and the natural world.

RELIGION

Oregon's Indians believed that powerful spirits ruled the natural world. Animals, rocks, plants, clouds, and the sun and moon all had spirits that could affect the lives of human beings. Because humans depended on nature for survival, they wanted to keep the spirits happy. When a hunter killed an elk or deer, he said a prayer to its spirit. He thanked it for dying and asked for others of its kind to come to the hunters as well.

Many rules, or **taboos,** surrounded the killing of game and preparation of food. When a young hunter

THE HUNTER AND THE ELK SPIRIT

Wascos told the story of a young hunter who met the spirit of the elk. The elk promised to be the young man's guardian, as long as he never killed more elk than he needed. For a time, the hunter was successful and brought plenty of meat back to the village. But his father complained that he should bring even more food. The young hunter set out and killed five whole herds of elk! Seeing this, the elk spirit declared he would no longer be the hunter's guardian. The hunter returned to his village and died in despair.

WORD TO KNOW

taboos *rules about how activities such as hunting and preparing food must be performed*

Picture Yourself . . .

in a Chinook Village

All morning you have been waiting at the river's edge. Again and again you look upstream, but there is no sign of the canoes that will bring the fishermen. You help your mother and the other women tend the cooking fires, and listen to the talk about the salmon runs of past years. "Someday the salmon won't come back," grumbles one old grandmother. "The way people behave these days, the salmon spirit is going to get angry and punish us all!"

Suddenly, you hear a shout and the rhythmic swish of paddles. You rush with the others to the riverbank and watch the canoes gliding toward you. They are heavy in the water, laden with the day's catch. You know that the salmon spirit is happy and your people will have plenty of food for another year.

FAQ ★ ★

Q: WHAT WERE SOME TABOOS?

A: Taboos of all types varied from place to place. Here are a few about catching salmon: A fisherman must not jump or step over the net. He must not cut up the first-caught salmon of the year until the afternoon. The drying of salmon must begin at the high tide. Murderers, people who prepare corpses for burial, widows, and widowers must not eat the first catch of the season.

killed his first deer, for example, he could not eat it himself. Instead, he was required to offer the meat to the elderly people of the village. Among some groups, meat had to be cut up and cooked in specific ways. Taboos could be very complex, and they varied from one village to another. Underlying many of these taboos was the belief that humans relied on nature and should be respectful of it.

HOOFPRINTS ON THE GRASSLANDS

In the late 1680s, bands of horses escaped from Spanish settlements in northern New Mexico. The horses found excellent grazing on the grassy plains, and their numbers quickly increased. In the next few decades, they spread northward. By the 1720s, they reached the Columbia Plateau.

It didn't take the Indians long to discover that horses were useful and valuable. Nez Perces, Cayuses, and Umatillas became expert at catching, taming, and riding horses. On horseback, they could travel great distances for trade and warfare. A man who owned many horses was wealthy and admired. As some men acquired more and more horses, while others had few, there was a greater gap between rich and poor within a community. The introduction of horses made villages more vulnerable to raids by other Native peoples. It was difficult to defend against a quick-striking attack by horseback.

The arrival of horses brought great changes to the people of eastern Oregon. Yet few could imagine the far greater changes that lay ahead.

A Nez Perce man on horseback

THE WOMAN WHO SAW THE WHITE MEN

Watkuweis (mid-1700s–early 1800s) grew up in a Nez Perce village. Blackfoot warriors from what is now Idaho captured her and traded her to Native Americans farther east. Eventually, she married a white man. A white doctor cured her of an eye disease that had taken much of her sight. When Watkuweis made her way back to Nez Perce land many years later, she told them about the people who had been kind to her. When the first white visitors reached Oregon and met with the Nez Perce people in 1805, they received a warm welcome.

READ ABOUT

This painting depicts the *Golden Hind*, the ship that Sir Francis Drake sailed up the Pacific coast.

1543

A Spanish ship sails up the Pacific coast, possibly to what is now southern Oregon

1792 ▲

Robert Gray becomes the first American to see the mouth of the Columbia River

1805–06

Lewis and Clark spend the winter at Fort Clatsop near the mouth of the Columbia River

EXPLORATION AND SETTLEMENT

CHAPTER THREE

EXPLORATION AND SETTLEMENT

★

AROUND 1543, A SPANISH SHIP SAILED ALONG THE COAST OF CALIFORNIA AND MIGHT HAVE REACHED SOUTHERN OREGON. The region didn't seem to have any gold, so the captain saw no reason to explore any farther. In 1577, British captain Sir Francis Drake sailed in the region. He was turned back by what he described as "vile, thick, stinking fogs." Still, he claimed the Pacific lands north of California for England.

1811
Fort Astoria becomes the first permanent U.S. settlement on the Pacific coast

1840s ▲
Thousands of people travel to Oregon along the Oregon Trail

1848
Oregon Territory is formally established.

Exploration of Oregon

The colored arrows on this map show the routes taken by explorers and pioneers between 1775 and 1830.

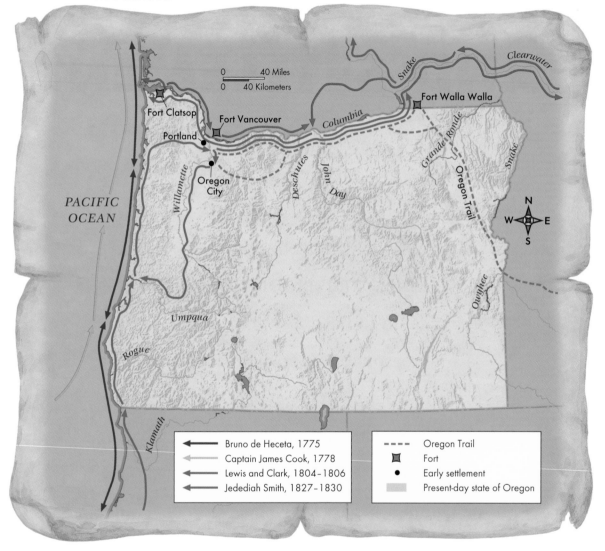

THE FUR TRADE

At first, Europeans paid little attention to Oregon because it had no resources they wanted. That suddenly changed in the late 1700s, when Chinese merchants began paying high prices for sea otter pelts. Russians traded for these

Fur trading at Fort Nez Perce

pelts with the Native people of Alaska and sailed their cargoes across the Pacific to China. Oregon was rich in sea otters, and soon British traders were encouraging Indians in the area to trade the glossy otter pelts for guns, kettles, beads, blankets, and rum.

Back east, the United States was also eager to trade with China. In 1787, the first American merchant ships left Boston, Massachusetts, for China. They sailed all the way around the southern tip of South America and then up the Pacific coast. They stopped at Oregon and Washington to trade for fur pelts before heading across the Pacific.

In 1788, the British North West Company began establishing trading posts in what is now British Columbia, Canada. Indians brought furs to the trading posts and exchanged them for guns and other goods. The sea otter

Glass beads traded between the British and Native Americans

trade transformed life for many coastal people. Instead of fishing and hunting for food, young men turned to otter hunting. The task could be dangerous. One British trader wrote, "Sometimes [Indians] surprise [the sea otter] sleeping on his back, on the surface of the water; and, if they can get near the animal without awakening him, . . . he is easily harpooned and dragged to the boat, when a fierce battle very often ensues between the otter and the hunters, who are frequently wounded by the claws and teeth of the animal."

Hunters slaughtered sea otters in staggering numbers. In just one year, between 1801 and 1802, traders shipped some 11,000 pelts to China from the North Pacific coast. As a result of overhunting, sea otters began to disappear from the Oregon coast. There was still a demand for pelts, so fur traders encouraged the Indians to trap minks, foxes, river otters, and muskrats. Beaver colonies thrived in Oregon's inland forests and streams. Beaver soon replaced sea otter as Oregon's most treasured pelt. And, like the sea otter, the beaver began to disappear.

THE CORPS OF DISCOVERY

For more than a century, France had claimed the land from today's Louisiana to the Dakotas and Montana. In 1803, President Thomas Jefferson bought this land in a $15 million deal known as the Louisiana Purchase. With the Louisiana Purchase, the size of the United States had suddenly doubled.

Jefferson was eager to learn about the territory and to establish claims to the land still farther west. In 1803, he picked a Virginia army officer, Meriwether Lewis, to head an exploring expedition. Lewis asked a fellow army officer, William Clark, to help lead the expedi-

Robert Gray

A MIGHTY RIVER

In 1792, a Boston merchant and sea captain named Robert Gray sailed up the Oregon coast, exploring inlets and bays. During his explorations, he came across a great river emptying into the sea. He named it the Columbia, after his ship, the *Columbia Rediviva*. No river in the Americas dumps more water into the Pacific Ocean than the powerful Columbia. Ironically, Gray was not impressed by what he saw. In his log, he wrote that the river "was not worthy of our further attention."

Sacagawea with explorers Meriwether Lewis and William Clark

tion. They recruited many men along the Ohio River on America's western frontier to join them in what was called the Corps of Discovery. The band of 33 explorers included Sacagawea, a young Shoshone woman. She spoke several American Indian languages. She served as ambassador when the Corps of Discovery met northwestern Native peoples, many of whom provided vital assistance to the expedition.

Jefferson had instructed Lewis and Clark to follow the Missouri River west and to search for a reliable and easy, as well as preferably all-water, route to the Pacific. They followed the Missouri River to its source on today's Montana-Idaho border. From there, they followed the Clearwater and Snake rivers, and finally reached the Columbia. In December 1805, the Corps of Discovery built a rough fort near the mouth of the Columbia. The explorers spent the winter at this fort, which they named Fort Clatsop.

Lewis and Clark made careful notes about the site's relentless fog and rain. During their three-month stay, they had only six days of sunshine! To add to their misery, their clothes and bedding were alive with fleas; many men came down with flu-like illnesses that lasted for months; and, during the winter, elk and pemmican were just about the only things to eat. Out of desperation, they tried another dish that the Indians recommended: dog meat. Clark disliked it, but Lewis wrote in his journal, "I think it an agreeable food and would prefer it vastly to lean venison or elk."

Despite their troubles and their disappointment in not finding an all-water route, Lewis and Clark returned with glowing reports about Oregon's promise. It was rich in furs, fish, and timber, and the grasslands of the Willamette Valley looked like perfect farming country.

A view of Astoria, at the mouth of the Columbia River, established by John Jacob Astor's Pacific Fur Company

THE ASTORIA ADVENTURE

In 1810, John Jacob Astor, a rich New York businessman, founded the Pacific Fur Company. He sent two expeditions to the Columbia River, one by land and the other by sea. When the oceangoing expedition reached Oregon in 1811, eight crew members drowned in high seas at the mouth of the Columbia River. The survivors awaited the overland expedition. Finally, in January 1812, the first members of the overland expedition arrived, weary and half-starved.

John Jacob Astor

Astor's men built a trading post called Astoria at the mouth of the Columbia. Indians arrived with furs, eager to trade with the newcomers. Just as things seemed to be going well, the Astorians learned that the United States and Great Britain were at war and that a British warship was on the way to attack them! Untrained and poorly armed, they knew they could not hold out against the British. The Pacific Fur Company sold its property to the British North West Company, which took over Astoria and renamed it Fort George. The United States went on to win the War of 1812, but Astor's dream of an American fur-trading empire never came true.

Over the next several years, Fort Astoria changed hands a number of times and was controlled by British, Canadian, and American traders. Eventually the British won out, and the Hudson's Bay Company began turning a huge profit. In exchange for furs, the company brought manufactured goods to Native villages along the Pacific coast and up to Alaska. The company also operated a lumber mill and began clearing land throughout the region. Next, the Hudson's Bay Company established Fort Vancouver along the Willamette and Columbia rivers. Slowly, the Chinooks and Clatsops found their homes and their lives to be changing.

Astoria was the first permanent U.S. settlement on the Pacific coast.

CAPTURING THE MOMENT

As European and American settlers moved into Oregon, painters tried to capture the beauty of the land and the experiences of the people. During the 1840s, English artist Henry Warre painted detailed pictures of the settlement at Oregon City. John Mix Stanley painted a portrait of John McLoughlin, the "Father of Oregon." Stanley pioneered the use of photography to capture the changing lives of Oregon's Indians. Historic themes also inspired sculptor Alice Cooper. Her bronze statue of Sacagawea stands today in Portland's Washington Park.

This painting, *The American Village*, by Henry Warre, depicts Oregon City in 1849.

MINI-BIO

JOHN McLOUGHLIN: THE "FATHER OF OREGON"

John McLoughlin (1784–1857) grew up in Canada and studied medicine as a young man. He served as a doctor at a fur-trading post and then became a trader himself. In 1824, he moved to the Oregon country to serve as head trader of the British-owned Hudson's Bay Company. His position afforded him power, and he aided wagon-train settlers in the Willamette Valley and helped keep the peace between Americans and British. In 1957, the Oregon legislature gave McLoughlin the honorary title, "the Father of Oregon."

? Want to know more? See arcweb.sos.state.or.us/archives/50th/McLoughlin/mcloughlincareer.html

---

WESTWARD MOVEMENT

In 1811, a clerk with the Pacific Fur Company wrote a glowing description of the Willamette Valley, saying that the climate was "remarkably mild" and the valley possessed "a rich and luxuriant soil, which yields an abundance of fruits and roots." A few years later, a U.S. House of Representatives report claimed that the Willamette Valley was "a boundless extent of the most fertile soil on this continent."

By the 1830s, the young nation was expanding westward. Plows had cut furrows across Indiana, Illinois, and Iowa. Many Americans believed that the nation was meant to spread across the continent all the way to the

Pacific Ocean. They said that God wanted the United States to stretch from sea to sea. Some politicians seized on this idea, called Manifest Destiny, and used it to encourage westward expansion.

In 1834, a young Methodist minister named Jason Lee traveled west from Missouri to the Willamette Valley. He intended to bring Christianity to the Indians. Lee worked eagerly. He set up a church and a one-room school near a village of the Kalapuya Nation. But Indian men and women had their own religion and were not interested in the Bible. Lee traveled back to the East Coast to recruit help. He returned with a group of teachers, ministers, and doctors known as "Lee's reinforcements." They set up branch **missions** at The Dalles and in what is now northwestern Oregon.

While the **missionaries** worked to convert Kalapuyas, the Indians were dying of European diseases. For thousands of years, the people of the Pacific Northwest had had little contact with outsiders. Europeans brought new diseases, such as smallpox, measles, and typhoid. Native Americans had no natural **immunity** to fight these deadly diseases, which swept through village after village. Indians knew of many plants with healing powers. They tried them all, but nothing seemed to help. European diseases wiped out whole towns and villages. Historians believe that between 1770 and 1865, 80 to 90 percent of Oregon's Native people died of disease. When Lee finally left Oregon in 1843, he wrote, "There were more children in the mission grave yard . . . than alive."

As time passed, the missionaries became less concerned with teaching the Bible and more interested in farming. As their plows broke the land, the missionaries helped prepare the way for thousands of others who

Jason Lee

WORDS TO KNOW

missions *places created by a religious group to spread its beliefs*

missionaries *people who try to convert others to a religion*

immunity *natural protection against disease*

The Oregon Trail, an oil painting by Albert Bierstadt

WORD TO KNOW

emigrants *people who leave their homes to live in another land*

SEE IT HERE!

BARLOW TRAIL

Following the Oregon Trail with his family, Sam Barlow looked for a shortcut to avoid a raft trip down the Columbia. He discovered a route around the base of Mount Hood. Parts of the road were rough, and in one spot, wagons had to go down a steep slope. Barlow created a "wagon chute" lined with tree stumps. Ropes tied to the stumps were used to lower the wagons slowly. Today, you can hike what's now called Barlow Road and see the wagon chute, where some trees still bear the marks of ropes.

would follow. Most 19th-century Americans lived on farms. To them, few things were more valuable than good soil. Stories of the rich land in the Willamette Valley filled them with excitement.

By the 1840s, many farmers in the Midwest were lured by the promise of the Oregon country. Thousands sold their farms and packed up their belongings. They bought oxen and wagons and joined the stream of **emigrants** heading west. The emigrants traveled with their cows, horses, chickens, pigs, and dogs. There were so many wagons that the wheels ground tracks into the earth that could be seen for the next 100 years.

Emigrants followed a route called the Oregon Trail, traveling along rivers, across plains, and over mountains. They followed the Missouri, the Platte, and the Sweetwater rivers, before turning northwest along the Snake River. At last, they crossed the Blue Mountains in northeastern Oregon and then followed the Columbia. At The Dalles, they boarded rafts for the 60-mile (97 km) trip into the Willamette Valley, or they followed a toll road around the base of Mount Hood.

It could take six months for people from the Midwest to reach Oregon. Many died of smallpox and other diseases along the way. "This day has been insupportable!" a woman wrote in her diary as she crossed Wyoming. "The dust and heat [are] scarcely to be endured. I try to be brave but in times like these my spirit falters."

The hardships did not end when travelers reached the valley of their dreams. They had to build cabins for themselves and survive on what little food they could find or buy until they harvested their first crops. Lucy Ann Henderson remembered her first winter near present-day Salem, when she was 11 years old: "There was no floor in the cabin, just earth. There was a big fireplace. There was but one room. There was a big chest and Mother filled

In 1845, about 2,000 white settlers lived in the Willamette Valley. Just 15 years later, that number had soared to 52,000!

Picture Yourself . . .

on the Oregon Trail

You never knew your feet could hurt so much! You've been walking almost all day, except for half an hour this afternoon when you clambered aboard the wagon. As soon as the oxen started climbing the next hill, your father made you get down and walk again. Now the wagons have all come to a stop, the men have unyoked the teams, and you can enjoy the best part of the day. As your mother and the other women set to work cooking supper, you slip away to look for your friend Sarah two wagons ahead. Sarah says she heard the men talking about a shortcut through the mountains. It will get you to the valley in just 10 more days! You prop your aching feet on a rock and wonder how you will walk one more day, let alone 10! Then you hear your mother calling you to help her stir the pot on the fire. You walk back, your feet throbbing with every step. You ask yourself why your family ever left Indiana. The Willamette Valley better be as good as they say!

this nearly full with clothing, and [my sister] Betty and I slept in that. . . . We lived on boiled wheat and boiled peas that winter."

The opening of the Oregon Trail had a disastrous impact on Oregon's Native Americans. The thousands of newcomers killed their game and pushed them off their land. Hoping to be left in peace, many Indians abandoned the Willamette Valley for less-desirable areas.

OREGON BECOMES AMERICAN

In 1843, William Overton of Tennessee and Asa Lovejoy of Boston, Massachusetts, began clearing land on the Willamette River, near where it flows into the Columbia. Overton soon sold his share of the claim to Francis Pettygrove of Portland, Maine. Lovejoy and Pettygrove each wanted to name the settlement after their home-towns. In 1845, they held a coin toss to decide the issue. Pettygrove won, and Portland was born. Before long, the town had a sawmill, a hotel, and a newspaper.

Like the sea otters before them, Oregon's foxes, beavers, and other fur-bearing animals were becoming scarce from relentless trapping. By the 1840s, the British-owned Hudson's Bay Company saw that there was no longer much profit in fur trading. At the same time, American emigrants were scooping up land in the Willamette Valley and crowding out the British.

In Washington, voices in Congress shouted that the United States should drive the British from the area known as Oregon Country, today called the Pacific Northwest. They argued that the U.S.-British boundary should be marked at latitude 54°40' W, which is well into present-day Canada. In 1844, James K. Polk was elected president on the slogan, "Fifty-four forty or fight!"

The British did not believe that Oregon was worth

LATITUDE AND LONGITUDE

Mapmakers draw grids on many maps and globes to serve as place markers. Longitude lines run north and south. Latitude lines run east and west, parallel to the equator. Each latitude line has a number based on its distance from the equator. The distance between these lines is measured in units called degrees and minutes, noted by the symbols ° and '.

MINI-BIO

JOE MEEK: SPEAKING FOR OREGON

fighting for, so they offered to make a compromise about the boundary line. They gave up their claim to what is now the northwestern United States, but did not agree to setting the boundary at 54° 40'. Instead, in 1846, British and U.S. officials signed an agreement establishing the 49th Parallel as the border between U.S. territory and British Canada. The U.S. portion of the Northwest was officially organized as the Oregon Territory in 1848. At last, the United States stretched from sea to shining sea.

As a young man, Joseph Lafayette Meek (1810–1875) spent more than 10 years roaming the Rocky Mountains, buying furs from the Indians. Eventually, he married the daughter of a Nez Perce chief and settled near present-day Hillsboro. In 1848, Meek went to Washington and met with President James K. Polk, whose wife was Meek's cousin. He urged Polk to make Oregon a U.S. territory. Meek later served as territorial federal marshal.

 Want to know more? See oregontrail.org/joe-meek-mountain-man-and-trapper.htm

A frontier town in what is now Oregon

READ ABOUT

A view of
First Street in
Portland, 1880s

1851 ▲
*Gold is found in
southern Oregon*

1851–56
*The Rogue River Wars
erupt between Indians
and white settlers*

▲**1859**
*Oregon becomes
the 33rd state in
the Union*

CHAPTER FOUR

GROWTH AND CHANGE

★

IN 1859, A NEWSPAPER IN PORTLAND LISTED THE SERVICES OF DOCTORS AND LAWYERS, DRUGGISTS AND BLACK-SMITHS. Carpenters, masons, and painters clamored for a place in the booming construction business. Dressmakers and dance teachers offered their talents. Oregon was thriving, and Portland was its bustling center.

1863 ▲
Oregon's first
railroad opens

1877
The Wallowa band of
Nez Perces refuses to
move to a reservation

1887
Whites murder 32
Chinese gold miners
on the Snake River

Digging for gold along Oregon's southern coast

GLITTERING DREAMS

When Oregon became a U.S. territory in 1848, cash was in short supply. Sometimes, people used bushels of wheat or pounds of sugar as money.

Then thrilling news reached the Willamette Valley. A sawmill overseer had discovered gold nuggets in northern California! Oregon farmers walked away from their plows and their half-tilled fields. The treasure of the Willamette Valley was nothing compared to the riches they imagined in the goldfields to the south.

By the end of 1848, about two-thirds of the white men in Oregon had left for California. Some of them struck it rich and returned with thousands of dollars in their pockets. Oregon's cash shortage was at an end. Instead of wheat and sugar, Oregonians began using gold dust as money. The territory even minted its own five- and ten-dollar gold coins with a picture of a beaver on the back. People called them Oregon Beavers.

In 1849, thousands of gold seekers poured into California from all over the world. Oregon farmers were quick to discover another way to strike it rich. California's gold miners were hungry for all the wheat, beef, apples, and eggs the farmers could produce. Heavily loaded wagons rumbled south. The southern Oregon towns of Jacksonville and Scottsburg sprouted up as supply centers for the wagon drivers.

In 1851, Oregon experienced a gold rush of its own. Gold seekers found pockets of gold in hills and streams in the southern part of the territory. Loose gold nuggets were even found on the beaches south of Coos Bay.

Oregon farmers produced wheat and other crops that gold miners needed.

DID OREGON WELCOME AFRICAN AMERICANS WHO WERE TRYING TO ESCAPE SLAVERY?

No. In fact, the territory passed a law forbidding African Americans from entering Oregon. This law, the result of racism, was unusual in the West. Most other western territories and states did not make such laws.

SLAVERY AND STATEHOOD

Oregon was a U.S. territory, but it was isolated from the country to which it belonged. Newspapers were several months old by the time they reached Portland. Nevertheless, Oregonians were keenly aware that the issue of slavery was dividing the country. For most white Southerners, slavery was an accepted part of life. Many people in the North, however, thought that slavery was unfair. They objected to how enslaved people were treated. There was also a concern that farmers who did not own slaves could not compete with landowners who were able to farm on a larger scale by using enslaved laborers. Most Oregonians opposed slavery because of the disadvantage it created for small-scale farmers and wanted it to be forbidden in the territory.

In 1857, the U.S. Supreme Court heard a case concerning an enslaved man named Dred Scott. In the Dred Scott decision, the Court ruled that Congress could not outlaw slavery in a U.S. territory. The only way Oregonians could keep slavery out was to apply for statehood.

On February 13, 1859, the U.S. Congress voted in favor of Oregon's application for statehood. The following day, Oregon became the 33rd state in the Union. The Willamette Valley town of Salem was established as the capital.

From 1861 to 1865, the United States fought the bloody Civil War. It put an end to slavery at last and kept 11 Southern states from permanently breaking away to form their own nation. Oregon sided with the Union but was affected very little by the war itself. Most fighting was far away, on the other side of the Rocky Mountains.

Oregon: From Territory to Statehood
(1848-1859)

This map shows the original Oregon territory and the area that became the state of Oregon in 1859.

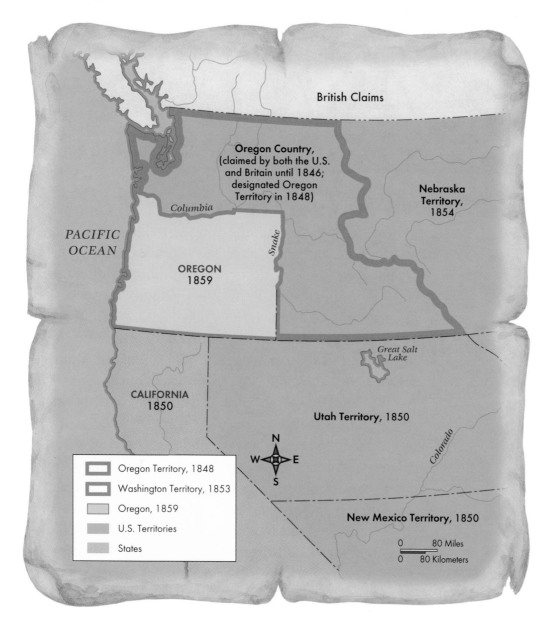

British Claims

Oregon Country, (claimed by both the U.S. and Britain until 1846; designated Oregon Territory in 1848)

Nebraska Territory, 1854

Columbia

Snake

PACIFIC OCEAN

OREGON 1859

Great Salt Lake

CALIFORNIA 1850

Utah Territory, 1850

Colorado

N
W E
S

Oregon Territory, 1848
Washington Territory, 1853
Oregon, 1859
U.S. Territories
States

New Mexico Territory, 1850

0   80 Miles
0   80 Kilometers

Paddle steamers, like this one on the Columbia River, helped Oregonians get their produce to market.

TO MARKET, TO MARKET

The gold rush led to the long-term development of northern California, and San Francisco arose as a major city. Californians needed lumber to build houses and food to put on their tables. Oregon eagerly sold Californians the goods they craved.

During the 1850s and 1860s, more and more farmers settled in southern Oregon. The soil of the Umpqua and Rogue river valleys proved excellent for growing wheat. By now, wheat was also the major crop in the Willamette Valley.

Native Americans had depended for centuries on the natural resources of the Umpqua and Rogue river valleys. As farmers poured in and seized this land, American Indians fought to defend it. From 1851 to 1856, American Indians and settlers fought a series of conflicts called the Rogue River Wars. Governor George Curry ordered that the Native Americans be killed on sight. Armed white men attacked American Indian villages, murdering women, children, and men as they slept.

The surviving Indians were eventually driven to the Grand Ronde and Siletz **reservations**. Although officials promised that the reservation land would belong to the Native Americans forever, the U.S. government whittled away these lands over the years. The American Indians were forced to live in unfamiliar places on poor farmland with little game or fish, and many died.

Until the 1850s, white settlement had not touched most of eastern Oregon. Then the search for gold led whites into the remote reaches beyond the Cascades. They found gold, and miners started moving into the area. Soon farmers realized that cattle and sheep could flourish on the sagebrush and grasses of the high plateau. Herds of steers and flocks of sheep grazed on land that people had once thought unfit for farming, providing food and goods for the miners.

As it grew, Oregon encouraged more people to come and settle. "We can offer the emigrant a civilization fresh in its newness," boasted a Willamette Valley newspaper in 1867. "We have forests for the lumberman of Maine, and fisheries for the fisherman of Cape Cod. . . . We have the soil whereon to settle hundreds of thousands."

In order to get their produce to market, Oregonians needed a speedy, reliable system of transportation. The Willamette, Columbia, and other rivers were natural shipping routes. Steamboat companies cleared and widened river channels so they could handle large vessels. In 1862, the Oregon Steam Navigation Company carried nearly 25,000 steamboat passengers.

In 1863, Oregonians saw their first railroad locomotives. A short rail line was built to carry goods and passengers overland around the Cascades and Celilo Falls of the

WORD TO KNOW

reservations *lands set aside for Native Americans to live on*

HENRY VILLARD: THE MAN WHO BUILT THE RAILROAD

In 1873, Henry Villard (1835–1900), a native of Germany, moved to Oregon, where he invested in the Northern Pacific Railway. He became president of the company in 1881. He donated millions of dollars to the newly established University of Oregon at Eugene. Villard also merged several East Coast electric companies. His new company later became General Electric.

Want to know more? See bluebook.state.or.us/notable/notvillard.htm

WORD TO KNOW

transcontinental *crossing an entire continent*

Columbia. Below the falls, they could catch a steamboat for the rest of the journey. People across the country cheered in 1869 when the first **transcontinental** railroad was completed. It linked the railway system of the eastern states with California. The trip across the Rockies once took six months of dangerous and exhausting travel. Now it was reduced to four high-speed days. In 1883, Portland was linked by rail to the transcontinental line, and this connection made it easier to ship goods from Oregon to many other parts of the United States. And Oregonians could read a newspaper from New York or Philadelphia the very week it was printed!

Laying track for the Union Pacific Railroad

The Union Pacific Railroad Company brought thousands of men from China to lay down track in California and Oregon. They worked tirelessly on a diet of rice and tea. Yet they received a hostile welcome in the United States. Some white workers accused them of driving down wages. Many Americans mistrusted the Chinese because their language and religion were different. During the 1880s, anti-Chinese gangs drove Chinese laborers out of Portland, Salem, Oregon City, and other towns. In the mid-1800s, many Chinese also came to Oregon to work as miners, but they faced discrimination. One observer wrote that Chinese miners "moved from mining locality to mining locality, fleeing from the kicks of one to the cuffs of another."

In 1887, 32 Chinese gold miners died in a cove on the Snake River in eastern Oregon. The miners were murdered by a group of white thieves who believed that the Chinese had struck it rich and buried a treasure near their camp.

FROM STREAMS TO FORESTS

For thousands of years, salmon provided food for Oregon's Native people. In the years after the Civil War, new Oregonians began to sell salmon for profit. New techniques for preserving and canning fish allowed

MINI-BIO

BETHENIA OWENS-ADAIR: MAKING HER OWN WAY

In 1843, Bethenia Owens-Adair (1840–1926) traveled from Missouri with her family on the Oregon Trail. After running a hat shop in Roseburg for six years, she went to Philadelphia to attend medical school. She returned to Oregon in 1881 and set up a successful medical practice in Portland. A few years later, she moved to Astoria and established her practice there. At that time, very few women worked as doctors. Owens-Adair boldly spoke out for women's rights and argued that women should be allowed to vote.

? Want to know more? See www.ohs.org/education/focus/breaking-tradition.cfm

Chinese workers at a salmon cannery near Astoria

During three months in 1894, a salmon wheel near The Dalles scooped 227,000 pounds (102,965 kg) of fish from the Columbia River.

companies to sell Columbia River salmon to markets as far away as England and Australia. Salmon were caught in huge nets that spanned streams and rivers. In some places, machines called salmon wheels scooped the fish out of the water with giant turning shovels.

At salmon-canning factories in Portland, The Dalles, and other growing cities, workers packed fresh salmon into 1-pound (0.45 kg) cans. Forty-eight cans were then packed into a single case for shipping. In 1866, Oregon shipped 4,000 cases of salmon. By 1887, that number had zoomed to 620,000!

The intensive fishing quickly depleted the salmon stock in the Columbia and other rivers. In 1894, an Oregon game official wrote, "For a third of a century

Oregon has drawn wealth from her streams, but now, by reason of her wastefulness and lack of intelligent provision for the future, the source of that wealth is disappearing."

Oregon's forests proved to be another source of wealth. A steam-powered machine called the log donkey hauled massive logs of pine and Douglas fir from the woods to nearby railways. Logging was especially heavy along rivers and railroad lines, which carried the raw timber to the sawmills. The mills sliced the logs into lumber to be shipped as far as the eastern United States and Europe.

A train transporting newly cut logs from Oregon forests

NATIVE AMERICAN ACTIVIST

Silas B. Smith (1840–1902) had a Clatsop mother and a white father, and he spent a lot of time among the Clatsop people during his early years. As a young man, he attended Dartmouth College in New Hampshire, where he earned a law degree. He returned to Oregon and set up a law practice in Astoria. He helped Oregon Indians fight to receive payment for their land from the federal government. He also wrote many articles celebrating the history and cultures of Native Americans of the Northwest.

A battle scene from the Nez Perce War of 1877

"I WILL FIGHT NO MORE FOREVER"

In 1855, a U.S. treaty granted the Nez Perce people a permanent reservation in Wallowa Valley, part of their traditional homeland. But, greedy for the Indians' lush grazing land, white ranchers pressured the government to move the Nez Perce people to a reservation in Idaho. In 1877, the American Indians received word that they would have to move. Many Nez Perce groups chose to live on the Idaho reservation, which was on another part of their traditional homeland. Some bands, whose ancestors had not traditionally lived in that region, refused to go, and war flared up.

A young chief named Hinmuuttu-yalatlat, or Thunder Rolling Down Mountain, led the Wallowa band of Nez Perces. The whites knew him as Joseph, a name Christian missionaries gave him as a boy. Fleeing from the U.S. Army, Chief Joseph led his people into the mountains. For four months, the army pursued Nez Perces across Idaho and into Montana. Chief Joseph hoped to lead his people across the Canadian border, where the army could not follow them. They were captured only 40 miles (64 km) from the border.

As he surrendered, Chief Joseph gave one of the saddest speeches in American history. "It is cold and we have no blankets," he said simply. "The little children are freezing to death. . . . I am tired. My heart is sick and sad. From where the sun now stands I will fight no more forever."

The Nez Perce War of 1877 was the last major Indian war in Oregon history. White people had taken over the land and would shape it to serve their purposes in the coming century.

FAQ

Q8 WHAT FINALLY BECAME OF THE WALLOWA NEZ PERCES?

A8 The army moved Chief Joseph's band to Kansas, then to present-day Oklahoma. In 1885, Chief Joseph and those who remained of his band were returned to the Pacific Northwest. Many of them lived on reservations of other Native groups and never saw the Wallowa Valley again.

Chief Joseph

WOMEN HAVE FULL SUFFRAGE IN

AUSTRALIA   NORWAY   ISLE OF MAN
NEW ZEALAND   FINLAND   TASMANIA

WOMEN HAVE MUNICIPAL
SUFFRAGE IN

ENGLAND   ICELAND   DENMARK
SCOTLAND   CANADA   SWEDEN
WALES   NATAL, SOUTH AFRICA

In the United States Women
Vote in twenty-eight states on
Municipal and School affairs

WOMEN VOTE
ON EQUAL TERMS WITH MEN

WYOMING   COLORADO
UTAH   WASHINGTON
IDAHO   CALIFORNIA

WHY NOT IN OREGON?

VOTE 300 X 'YES' AMENDMENT NO. 1, NOV. 6, 1912

1902

The Oregon constitution is changed to allow initiatives and referendums on the ballot

▲ 1912

Oregon women win the right to vote

1922

Oregon bars Japanese immigrants from purchasing land in the state

CHAPTER FIVE

MORE MODERN TIMES

★

IF YOU WALKED THROUGH PORTLAND IN 1900, YOU MIGHT HAVE HEARD A STREET VENDOR SINGING IN ITALIAN. You might have seen Chinese men talking on a busy corner. You might have seen an African American police officer on duty. You might have heard workers in a salmon-canning factory speaking in Russian. Oregon had become a promised land for people from other parts of the United States and around the world.

1937 ▶
The Bonneville Lock and Dam is completed on the Columbia River

1942–45
Vanport becomes the second-largest city in Oregon

2005
Oregon celebrates the bicentennial of the Corps of Discovery

A ZEAL FOR REFORM

Some new arrivals found work in the logging, fishing, and ranching industries. Many settled in Portland and took jobs in Oregon's factories and mills. Often they worked for low wages and lived in crowded, unhealthy conditions—while their employers grew wealthy in the railroad, logging, canning, and other industries.

Some Oregonians worked hard to help the state's poor. They opened hospitals and homes to care for orphans. They also challenged the system of voting. As in most states, Oregon voters elected representatives to the state legislature, expecting their representatives to support laws that would benefit the people. In 1902, Oregon changed its constitution to create a

A group of harvest workers resting on sacks of grain

new system. The "Oregon System" allowed people to vote directly on statewide issues in referendums. Voters could also place a possible law on the ballot as an initiative, or plan of action. This example of "direct democracy" proved important to the state and later to the nation.

Through initiatives and referendums, Oregon voters were able to bring about many reforms. They established homes for orphans and hospitals for the mentally ill. Voting soon became complicated as more and more referendums and initiatives were put on each ballot. Referendums and initiatives are still used today, though not as often as they once were.

Another major reform effort carried out in Oregon was one to secure full rights for women. In the years after the Civil War, people across the country tried to stop the sale of alcoholic beverages. This was called the temperance movement. In Oregon, women involved with the temperance movement burst into taverns and sang hymns to the customers.

Women realized that they would be better able to change the laws about drinking and other issues if they had the right to vote. In 1871, a former schoolteacher named Abigail Scott Duniway founded a newspaper that championed women's rights (Duniway did not support the temperance movement, but she felt it was impor-

WILLIAM SIMON U'REN: POWER TO THE PEOPLE

William Simon U'Ren (1859–1949) led Oregonians in the reform movement called populism, which sought to give greater power to the people. In 1902, he fought for and won a constitutional **amendment** that allowed citizens to place initiatives on the ballot and to vote for them directly by referendum. He also helped pass a 1908 amendment that gave voters the power to **recall** elected officials, and he helped establish the first primary election in the nation.

? **Want to know more?** See www.oregonlive.com/century/1900_index.html

WORDS TO KNOW

amendment *a change to a law or legal document*

recall *to remove elected officials from office*

In 1912, Oregon voters had so many referendums that the ballot measured 4.5 square feet (0.4 square meters)!

Delegates to the National American Woman Suffrage Association Convention in Portland, 1905

MINI-BIO

ABIGAIL SCOTT DUNIWAY: A VOICE FOR WOMEN'S RIGHTS

When she was 17, Abigail Scott Duniway (1834–1915) traveled by oxcart with her family from Illinois to Oregon. The long trip west showed her that women often endured the consequences of decisions made solely by men. Later, when she worked as a teacher, she discovered that women were paid far less than men for the same work. She became a local and national leader in the effort to win women the right to vote. Her hard work helped secure the vote for women in Oregon in 1912.

? Want to know more? See www.opb.org/oregonexperience/duniway/about.php

tant that women have equal rights). The following year, the Oregon legislature considered granting **suffrage** to women. The measure lost by only one vote. Oregon passed a law in 1878 that allowed women to own property. Women finally got the right to vote in Oregon in 1912, seven years before an amendment to the U.S. Constitution granted woman suffrage nationwide.

WORD TO KNOW

suffrage *the right to vote*

WARTIME AND BOOM TIME

In 1917, the United States entered World War I. Warships were in demand to fight the enemy at sea and to transport soldiers and supplies to the battlefields in Europe. Thousands of workers flocked to Portland to work in the shipping industry. Young men from Oregon's farms and factories signed up to fight overseas. When they returned, they brought stories of the world beyond their familiar fields and small towns.

Members of the "Portland Bunch," the 116th Depot Brigade, during World War I

At the end of the war, Oregonians in rural areas still lived much as their grandparents had. A man from Grants Pass remembered how his family built their own log cabin in 1918: "My mother and father had four iron wheels off some old washing machines. We made a crude log hauler and that's the only thing we had to haul those big logs on for the cabin! . . . My mother rived [cut] the shakes [shingles] for the roof as well as the barn and the chicken house."

In the 1920s, technological advancements brought radical changes. For the first time, electricity and running water reached Oregon's small towns and many isolated farms. The first telephone wires stretched above country roads.

Automobiles began to replace horse-drawn wagons. Hundreds of miles of rural roads were paved to make driving easier. When Oregonians got cars, they began to venture farther from home, much as Nez Perces had done when they tamed their first horses. During the 1920s, people drove to Oregon's beaches and mountains for weekend visits. Mountain climbing in the Cascades and Klamaths became a popular pastime.

Not all Oregonians enjoyed the good times of the

This photograph shows a gathering of Ku Klux Klan members meeting at the Lane County Rodeo Arena in the early 1920s.

1920s, however. Oregon was still unfriendly toward many people. The Alien Land Act of 1922 made it illegal for immigrants from Japan to buy land in the state. A white supremacist organization called the Ku Klux Klan spread hatred and sometimes used violence against Catholic immigrants, Asians, Jews, and African Americans. The Klan tried to shut down Catholic schools and to discourage African Americans from settling in Oregon. By 1924, the Klan fell out of favor when Oregonians saw the corruption of its leaders.

HARD TIMES AND WARTIME

In 1929, the New York stock market crashed, throwing the country further into the Great Depression. Banks and factories closed, and millions of people across the country lost their jobs. Oregon farmers had to sell their wheat and beef for a fraction of what they were worth a few years before.

During the Depression, President Franklin D. Roosevelt established government programs called the New Deal to create jobs for thousands of Americans. In Oregon, young men hired by the Civilian Conservation Corps (CCC) developed parkland for public use. (The CCC was not open to women.) The Works Progress Administration hired men and women as writers, artists, and photographers to document Oregon life and history. Most Oregonians welcomed the programs and were glad to have the jobs they created, but some people grumbled that the programs were a waste of money. In 1936, Oregon governor Charles Henry Martin complained that the country had "lost its moral force through pampering its people." Martin was not reelected.

In 1937, Japan invaded China, kicking off World War II in Asia. On December 7, 1941, Japanese planes bombed the U.S. naval fleet stationed at Pearl Harbor in the Hawaiian Islands, forcing the United States to enter the war. People in Oregon worried that the Japanese would attack the U.S. mainland next and that the Oregon coast would be a prime target. Many people

SEE IT HERE!

BONNEVILLE DAM

In 1933, the federal government began the Bonneville Lock and Dam, a massive construction project on the Columbia River. Completed in 1937, the dam spans the river 40 miles (64 km) east of Portland at the Columbia River Gorge. The lock and dam generate electrical power for Oregon and Washington, and make it easier for large ships to travel on the lower Columbia. The dam created a large reservoir known as Lake Bonneville. The dam has 18 spillway gates over a length of 1,450 feet (442 m), which allow water to be released. A new lock opened to replace the original one in 1993.

CCC workers planting seedlings on an Oregon hillside in 1939

Q8 DID THE JAPANESE EVER ATTACK THE MAINLAND UNITED STATES?

A8 On June 21, 1942, a Japanese submarine lobbed shells at Fort Stevens near the mouth of the Columbia River. The fort was undamaged in the attack. On May 5, 1945, a Japanese bomb carried by a balloon killed a woman and five children who were picnicking near Lakeview in southern Oregon. They were the only civilian casualties of the war on the U.S. mainland.

WORDS TO KNOW

internment camps *places where people are confined, usually during wartime*

segregated *separated from others according to race, class, ethnic group, religion, or other factors*

During World War II, the shipbuilding center of Vanport was the second-biggest city in Oregon.

also feared that Japanese Americans living on the West Coast might be spies for the Japanese government.

In February 1942, President Roosevelt signed an order sending Japanese Americans along the West Coast to **internment camps** farther inland. With only a few weeks' notice, thousands of loyal American citizens were forced to leave their homes, schools, and jobs and placed in camps surrounded with barbed wire. Meanwhile, many young Japanese American men fought in Europe and died for the United States during the war.

World War II pulled the United States out of the Depression. The government poured vast amounts of money into the military, and the country went back to work making everything from ships to uniforms. Camp Adair near Corvallis became a bustling army training facility. The Kaiser Shipyards near Portland went into high gear. They turned out a 10,000-ton "liberty ship" every 10 days. To house the thousands of shipyard workers and their families, the government created Vanport, a community of hastily built cottages north of Portland. Many of the shipyard workers who came to Oregon during the war were African Americans. Despite their hard work, African Americans continued to experience discrimination in the state. Housing in Vanport was **segregated** by race.

BUILDING THE FUTURE

Henry John Kaiser (1882–1967) was born in New York but moved to the Northwest in the early 1900s. In 1914, he started a road-building company, which soon became known for its excellent work. In 1931, he branched out into dam building. His company worked on the Hoover, Grand Coulee, and Bonneville dams. During World War II, Kaiser's company turned to shipbuilding and became a leader in the industry. One of his shipyards was located in Portland. After the war, he expanded into housing construction and built 10,000 new homes.

Another group of workers who arrived in Oregon during the war came from Mexico. Because so many U.S. men were away fighting the war, there was a great need for farmworkers. In 1942, the Mexican Farm Labor Program was begun as a way to bring "guest workers" to the United States. Also known as the bracero program, this system helped with the huge labor shortage. But many of the workers were treated badly and paid poorly. By the time the program ended in 1964, more than 15,000 Mexicans had settled in Oregon.

Mexican laborers picking potatoes in an Oregon field, 1943

BEATRICE MORROW CANNADY: CHANGING THE LAWS

When Beatrice Morrow Cannady (1890–1974) moved to Portland in 1910, she joined the city's small but active African American community. She and her husband edited the Advocate, the city's only African American newspaper. Eventually, she left newspaper work and earned a law degree. In 1925, she worked successfully to repeal Oregon's Black Laws. Dating back to territorial days, these laws said that African Americans could not settle in Oregon. Cannady moved to Los Angeles in the 1930s and lived there for the rest of her life.

❓ **Want to know more?** See www.opb.org/programs/oregonexperience/cannady

Oregonians of all ages protested development of beach areas in 1968.

RESPECTING THE LAND

World War II brought thousands of workers to Oregon. Once the war was over, many decided to live and work in Oregon's towns and cities. The state's natural beauty enchanted many of these new Oregonians. They enjoyed hiking, canoeing, mountain climbing, and other outdoor activities.

In the 1960s and 1970s, Oregon lawmakers acted to protect and restore the environment. New laws limited the amount of logging allowed in state forests and required that new trees be planted. Volunteer crews, including thousands of schoolchildren, planted trees throughout the state.

New dams and irrigation projects brought water to the dry plateaus east of the Cascades. Apple and cherry orchards flourished on land that was once suitable only for grazing sheep and cattle.

In the 1980s, a slowdown in the construction business weakened Oregon's timber industry. Many logging operations and lumber mills shut down. The industry revived somewhat in the 1990s, but many lifelong loggers retired or moved on to other jobs. Tourism and the computer industry became increasingly important. But these industries have been more successful in urban areas than in rural ones. Many rural areas of the state continue to struggle economically.

Back in 1905, Oregon had celebrated the 100th anniversary (centennial) of the arrival of Lewis and Clark. All summer long, people flocked to the Lewis and Clark Centennial Exposition in Portland. Exhibits at the fair showed the progress Oregon had made in the past century and looked forward to greater gains in the future. Between 2003 and 2006, the National Park Service sponsored a number of events paying tribute to the 200th anniversary (bicentennial) of Lewis and Clark's journey. In 2005, the National Park Service established the Lewis and Clark National Historical Park, which has several sites along the Columbia River in Oregon. Like the centennial celebration before it, the Lewis and Clark Bicentennial remembered Oregon's history and honored the accomplishments of the Corps of Discovery for future generations to cherish.

Visitors at Fort Clatsop National Memorial, part of the Lewis and Clark National Historical Park

READ ABOUT

Greg Oden, the number-one 2007 NBA draft pick of the Portland Trail Blazers, signs autographs.

CHAPTER SIX

PEOPLE

★

O N AVERAGE, OREGON HAS 39 PEOPLE PER SQUARE MILE (15 PER SQUARE KILOMETER). New Jersey, in contrast, has about 1,000 people per square mile (386 per sq km). This doesn't mean that most Oregonians live in wide-open spaces. In fact, nearly half of the state's people are packed into and around the city of Portland. About 79 percent of all Oregonians live in cities. The rest live on farms or in towns of 2,500 people or less. Most rural people are farmers or ranchers living east of the Cascades.

Where Oregonians Live

The colors on this map indicate population density throughout the state. The darker the color, the more people live there.

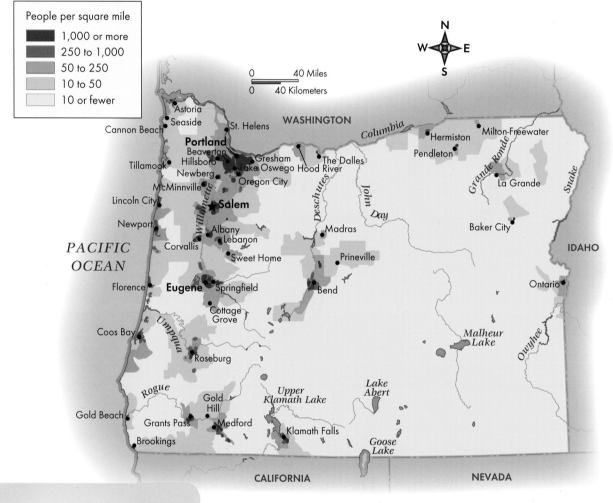

People per square mile

- 1,000 or more
- 250 to 1,000
- 50 to 250
- 10 to 50
- 10 or fewer

Big City Life

This list shows the population of Oregon's biggest cities.

Portland 537,081
Salem 152,239
Eugene 146,356
Gresham 97,105
Beaverton 89,643

Source: U.S. Census Bureau, 2006 estimate

WHO'S AN OREGONIAN?

Oregon values its reputation as a scenic state with friendly, open-minded people. The people of Oregon represent virtually every ethnic group and cultural background. They contribute a rich medley of music, food, arts, crafts, and literature to the state.

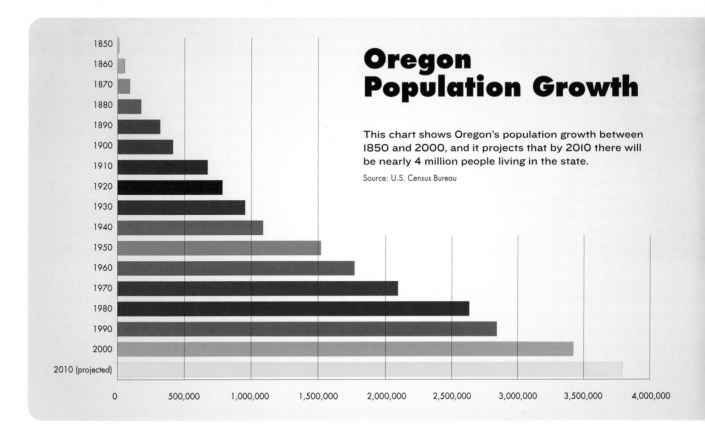

Oregon Population Growth

This chart shows Oregon's population growth between 1850 and 2000, and it projects that by 2010 there will be nearly 4 million people living in the state.

Source: U.S. Census Bureau

People QuickFacts

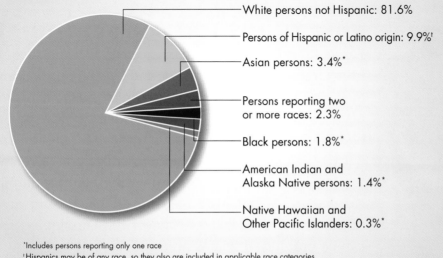

White persons not Hispanic: 81.6%

Persons of Hispanic or Latino origin: 9.9%†

Asian persons: 3.4%*

Persons reporting two or more races: 2.3%

Black persons: 1.8%*

American Indian and Alaska Native persons: 1.4%*

Native Hawaiian and Other Pacific Islanders: 0.3%*

*Includes persons reporting only one race
†Hispanics may be of any race, so they also are included in applicable race categories
Source: U.S. Census Bureau, 2005 estimate

Shopping at a farmers market in Eugene

HOW TO TALK LIKE AN OREGONIAN

East of the Cascades, the phrase "I reckon" is often heard, and people tend to say "at any rate" where people in other parts of the country might say "anyway." Some people use the word *necklet* for necklace. Sometimes, colorful phrases slip into ordinary conversation. If a child throws away part of her meal, her grandmother might comment, "You'll see the time when you'll follow the crows a mile for that!" If someone puts on airs, an Oregonian might remark, "There she goes, head up and tail a-risin'!"

HOW TO EAT LIKE AN OREGONIAN

For thousands of years, Indians lived on fish and shellfish from Oregon's coast and rivers, and Oregonians continue to savor their seafood. They also enjoy fresh farm products, including hazelnuts, berries, dairy products, and honey. Oregon pears are known throughout the world.

Oregon chefs have developed hundreds of recipes for dishes made with homegrown ingredients. Salmon can be served baked, grilled, or fried, with an array of mouthwatering sauces. The prized Dungeness crab can be purchased live or precooked.

Dungeness crab

MENU

WHAT'S ON THE MENU IN OREGON?

★ ★ ★

Carton of blueberries

The Dungeness Crab

Dungeness crabs live along the Pacific coast from Alaska to northern California. On the Oregon coast, they grow to be about 8 inches (20 cm) long. Eating crabs takes patience, as some of the sweetest meat has to be picked out of the shell with tongs and fingers. Don't worry about getting your hands messy—just enjoy the feast!

Seafood chowder

This delicious dish is a thick combo of fish, clams, potatoes, and vegetables.

Cedar plank salmon

Grilling salmon on a plank of red cedar gives it a deep, smoky flavor. The cedar plank is moistened for 24 hours to keep it from burning.

Fresh pear and goat cheese salad

Sliced pears and chunks of goat cheese nestle on a bed of greens. The salad is garnished with nuts and raisins.

Pear and goat cheese salad

TRY THIS RECIPE
Very Berry Cobbler

An array of desserts make use of Oregon's hazelnuts, blueberries, blackberries, and raspberries. Try this one for Very Berry Cobbler (and be sure to have a grown-up nearby to help):

Ingredients:
FILLING
5 cups berries of any combination: raspberries, blackberries, blueberries, boysenberries, or sliced strawberries
⅓ cup sugar
1 tablespoon flour
Splash of lemon juice (optional)

DOUGH
1½ cups flour
1 teaspoon baking powder
¼ teaspoon baking soda
1 tablespoon sugar
4 tablespoons unsalted butter, chilled

Instructions:
1. Preheat oven to 375°.
2. In a 10- or 12-inch glass pie plate, mix the berries, sugar, flour, and lemon juice (if using).
3. Bake for 30 minutes, stirring once. Remove from the oven.
4. To make the dough, stir the flour, baking powder, baking soda, and sugar together in a medium-sized bowl.
5. Grate the butter with a cheese grater and combine into the dough mixture with a fork or with your hands.
6. When the mixture is thoroughly combined, drop it in 6 large spoonfuls over the berries.
7. Bake for 20 minutes.

GOING TO SCHOOL

Under Oregon law, children between the ages of seven and 17 must attend school. Most Oregon children go to public school. Some attend private schools, and a growing number are homeschooled.

Willamette University in Salem held its first classes in 1842. The publicly funded University of Oregon in Eugene and Portland State University are the biggest universities in the state. Other state-supported schools include Oregon State University in Corvallis and Southern Oregon State College in Ashland. Among Oregon's many private colleges are Linfield College in McMinnville, Lewis & Clark College in Portland, Pacific University in Forest Grove, Reed College in Portland, and the University of Portland.

WORKS OF BEAUTY

During the 1930s, Harry Wentz of The Dalles painted vivid watercolors inspired by Oregon's mountains and rugged coast. Clayton "C. S." Price painted scenes of horses, cattle, and cowboy life. Both Wentz and Price taught painting at a school sponsored by the Portland Art Association. The Portland Center for the Visual Arts, which opened in 1972, displays the work of many of the state's finest painters and sculptors.

Marie Watt is a sculptor who lives and works in Portland and teaches art at Portland Community College. Part

MINI-BIO

PIETRO BELLUSCHI: DESIGNING HOUSES TO SUIT THE LAND

Soon after World War I, Pietro Belluschi (1899–1994) moved from Italy to the United States. In 1925, he settled in Portland, where he took a job with a leading architectural firm. Belluschi wanted to design buildings that fit Oregon's natural landscape. His wide, low houses, both simple and spacious, represent his Oregon style. Among his best-known buildings are the Portland Art Museum and the library at Reed College. Belluschi taught architecture at the Massachusetts Institute of Technology (MIT) from 1951 to 1973. He spent his final years in Portland, where he was honored for his lasting contributions.

❓ **Want to know more?** See bluebook.state.or.us/notable/notbelluschi.htm

Students in a Beaverton classroom

of her series *Blanket Stories* consists of two towers of folded blankets, many of which were traded to the Native Americans by the Hudson's Bay Company in the 19th century.

TELLING TALES

The legendary past of Oregon's first people forms the backdrop for the 1891 novel *The Bridge of the Gods*, by Frederic Homer Balch. In the 20th century, some Oregon writers drew upon the adventures of the state's white pioneers. In his

MINI-BIO

BEVERLY CLEARY: INVENTING RAMONA

When she was growing up, Beverly Cleary (1916–) didn't enjoy reading. She longed for books about children like herself and her classmates. In 1950, she began to fill this gap by publishing her first novel for young people, *Henry Huggins*. For more than 50 years, her books about ordinary kids have delighted readers all over the world. Among her best-loved characters are Henry Huggins, his friend Beezus Quimby, and Beezus's little sister, Ramona. Cleary was born in McMinnville and lived in Portland for most of her life. Most of her stories take place on Klickitat Street, a fictional street in an Oregon town. Statues of Ramona, Henry, and Henry's dog, Ribsy, stand today in Portland's Grant Park.

? Want to know more? See www.beverlycleary.com

MINI-BIO

URSULA K. LE GUIN: CREATING NEW WORLDS

Ursula K. Le Guin (1929–) has the gift of imagination, combined with a desire to help readers reexamine themselves and what's important to them. She grew up in California and moved to Portland in 1958. Many of her novels portray alien cultures, which mirror our own in startling ways. In 1969, her novel *The Left Hand of Darkness* won the Hugo and Nebula awards for fantasy and science fiction. LeGuin is the author of several books for children, including *Catwings* (1988) and *Jane on Her Own* (1999).

? Want to know more? See www.cbcbooks.org/cbcmagazine/meet/leguin_ursula_k.html

Jon Krakauer, author of *Into Thin Air*

1935 novel *Honey in the Horn*, H. L. Davis describes farming on the high plateau. Mary Jane Carr depicts the lives of pioneer children in her young adult novel *Children of the Covered Wagon*. Don Berry's 1960 novel *Trask* is about a mountain man's quests in the rain forests and rugged headlands of the Oregon coast.

Oregon serves as the setting for two classic novels by Ken Kesey, who grew up in Springfield. *One Flew over the Cuckoo's Nest* (1962) is set in a large state-run institution for the mentally ill. Oregon's logging country is the setting for *Sometimes a Great Notion* (1964).

The poetry of Lawson Fusao Inada reflects the culture of Japanese Americans on the West Coast. Inada, who taught at Southern Oregon University, spent the World War II years in a detention camp, and this experience is conveyed in many of his poems. He was named Oregon's Poet Laureate in 2006.

A deep love of the outdoors inspires many Oregon writers. Barry Lopez reflects on humans and their relationship with nature in three books of essays: *Desert Notes*, *River Notes*, and *Field Notes*. Both children and adults can enjoy his short novel *Crow and Weasel*. Mountain climbing is a passion for Jon Krakauer of Corvallis. His 1997 best seller, *Into Thin Air*, tells the story of a disastrous expedition to scale Mount Everest.

Miranda July earned praise for her film *Me and You and Everyone We Know.*

Miranda July is a filmmaker and short-story writer. She moved to Portland in the early 1990s and lived there for several years. Her 2005 independent film, *Me and You and Everyone We Know,* won a major prize at the Cannes Film Festival in France. Her 2007 short-story collection, *No One Belongs Here More than You,* won the Frank O'Connor International Short Story Award.

VOICES AND IMAGES

In the world of comics and cartoons, several Oregonians are among the best known. Mel Blanc of Portland earned the nickname the Man of a Thousand Voices for his perfor-

MINI-BIO

CARL BARKS: DUCKBURG DAYS

For many years, Carl Barks (1901–2000) drifted from job to job in and around Grants Pass. He had always been artistic, but his talent didn't pay off until he started drawing for the comic-book industry in the 1940s. In words and pictures, he created Duckburg, the home of Donald Duck, his three nephews, and his money-clutching Uncle Scrooge. Donald Duck's ill-fated efforts to find a steady job recall Barks's own years of hapless drifting.

? Want to know more?
See www.upress.state.ms.us/books/98

mances in radio comedies of the 1930s and 1940s. He could sound like a squawking parrot, a whinnying horse, or an old car in need of a tune-up. Blanc went on to do the voices of Bugs Bunny, Tweety Bird, Porky Pig, Barney Rubble in *The Flintstones*, and a host of other cartoon characters.

Matt Groening grew up in Portland and moved to California after he finished college. In 1977, he started a comic-strip magazine that attracted the attention of a TV producer, who invited him to develop a new cartoon show. Groening's series *The Simpsons* began its run on Fox TV in 1989. His stories of the Simpson

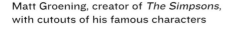

Matt Groening, creator of *The Simpsons*, with cutouts of his famous characters

family poke fun at American politics, consumerism, media idols, fashions, and just about everything else! Groening named many of his characters, including Homer and Marge Simpson, after members of his own family. The Simpsons and their friends live in a western town called Springfield, which resembles Springfield, Oregon.

Another Oregon cartoonist is John Callahan of Portland. At the age of 21, Callahan was injured in a car accident and became **quadriplegic**. He draws by holding a pen between his hands. Callahan's cartoons find humor in disability and other topics usually thought too sensitive for comedy. He has written two memoirs: *Don't Worry, He Won't Get Far on Foot* and *Will the Real John Callahan Please Stand Up?*

A number of Oregonians have become famous in the field of music. Obo Addy teaches at Lewis & Clark College in Portland. Addy was born in Ghana, West Africa, where he learned traditional drumming and chants from his father. He blends Ghanaian traditional music with Western melodies and instruments to create a musical form he calls world beat. Addy founded Homowo African Arts and Cultures, an organization that sponsors an annual festival in Oregon.

TAKING ON CHALLENGES

Many Oregonians spend their weekends and vacations hiking, canoeing, mountain climbing, kayaking, or white-water rafting. Others excel in athletics. Danny Ainge of Eugene played with several NBA teams, including the Boston Celtics and the Phoenix Suns. He played with the Portland Trail Blazers, Oregon's only major professional sports team, from 1990 to 1992. He was inducted into the Oregon Sports Hall of Fame in 1999.

SEE IT HERE!

OREGON SHAKESPEARE FESTIVAL

Every summer, thousands of theater lovers flock to Ashland in southern Oregon for its Shakespeare festival. Costumes and sets look much as they did in the England of Shakespeare's time. Many plays are performed in an outdoor theater with the mountains in the background.

WORD TO KNOW

quadriplegic *totally or partially paralyzed from the neck down*

Obo Addy

American runner Steven Prefontaine leads the pack during a race at the 1972 Summer Olympics.

While he was at the University of Oregon, Bill Bowerman trained 31 Olympic athletes and 16 runners who ran the 4-minute mile.

Bill Bowerman coached the track-and-field program at the University of Oregon in Eugene from 1948 to 1972, turning it into one of the best track-and-field programs in the world. On a trip to New Zealand in 1962, Bowerman saw people jogging for fun and exercise. He wrote articles and books about jogging when he returned to the United States. Before long, the whole nation was off and running!

One of the most gifted runners Bowerman ever trained was Steven Prefontaine of Coos Bay. Prefontaine, affectionately known as "Pre," won world records in various distance running categories, from 1,000 meters to 10,000 meters. His career was cut short when he died in a car accident at the age of 24 in 1975.

Another outstanding Oregon runner is Mary Decker Slaney. At age 15, "Little Mary Decker" won the 800-meter dash in a competition at Minsk in present-day Russia. Decker Slaney went on to break numerous world records in the early 1980s. In 2003, she was inducted into the U.S. Track & Field Hall of Fame.

Mary Decker Slaney runs a qualifying heat at the 1998 Summer Olympics.

MINI-BIO

LARRY MAHAN: RIDE 'EM COWBOY!

When he was growing up in Salem, horses and cowboys fascinated Larry Mahan (1942–). At 14, he entered his first rodeo and launched an impressive career. He became a champion at bull riding, bronco-busting, and many other daring rodeo events. From 1966 to 1970, and again in 1973, he was the World All-Around Rodeo Champion. He was inducted into the Oregon Sports Hall of Fame in 1985.

? Want to know more?
See www.larrymahan.com

READ ABOUT

The state senate prepares for a vote in 2005.

CHAPTER SEVEN

GOVERNMENT

★

IN 1857, OREGONIANS APPROVED A STATE CONSTITUTION, OR BODY OF LAWS, WHICH STILL GOVERNS THEM TODAY. The legislature can make amendments to the constitution with the approval of the voters. An amendment can also be placed on the ballot and approved directly by the people in an election. This direct voting is permitted because of the tradition of initiatives and referendums, which dates all the way back to 1902.

90

MINI-BIO

EDITH STARRETT GREEN: EDUCATION FIRST!

Edith Starrett Green (1910–1987) grew up in a family of teachers, and education was important to her all her life. She represented her Oregon district in the U.S. Congress from 1954 to 1974. In Congress, education and women's rights were her main priorities, and she often said that education should be the nation's number-one concern. In 1963, she worked for the passage of a law that would have given women equal pay with men.

? Want to know more? See http://bioguide.congress.gov/scripts/biodisplay.pl?index=G000407

The state capitol in Salem

Capital City

This map shows places of interest in Salem, Oregon's capital city.

The pioneer statue on the Oregon state capitol is 23 feet (7 m) tall and weighs 8.5 tons!

Willamette River

22

SALEM

Historic Downtown Salem

Hallie Ford Museum of Art

Oregon State Capitol

Marion County Historical Society Museum

22

Mission Mill Museum

Bush House Museum

Historic Deepwood Estate

Oregon State Government

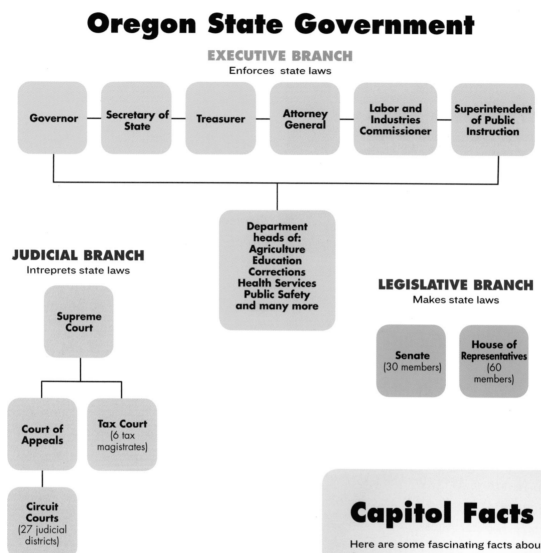

EXECUTIVE BRANCH
Enforces state laws

| Governor | Secretary of State | Treasurer | Attorney General | Labor and Industries Commissioner | Superintendent of Public Instruction |

Department heads of:
Agriculture
Education
Corrections
Health Services
Public Safety
and many more

JUDICIAL BRANCH
Intreprets state laws

Supreme Court

Court of Appeals

Tax Court
(6 tax magistrates)

Circuit Courts
(27 judicial districts)

LEGISLATIVE BRANCH
Makes state laws

Senate
(30 members)

House of Representatives
(60 members)

BRANCHES OF GOVERNMENT

Oregon's government is divided into three branches. The legislative branch makes the laws. The executive branch, or office of the governor, makes sure that the laws are followed. And the judicial branch, or court system, interprets the laws.

Capitol Facts

Here are some fascinating facts about Oregon's state capitol.

Height: 106 feet (32 m)
Opened: 1938
History: This is the third building to serve as the Oregon capitol. Fire destroyed the other two.
Interior: A bronze copy of the state seal is embedded in the floor.
Dome: Crowning the capitol's dome is a bronze statue of an Oregon pioneer covered with shiny gold leaf.

WEIRD AND WACKY LAWS

Oregon has some pretty silly laws. These are still on the books, but it's unlikely they're ever enforced:

- In Oregon kitchens, dishes must drip-dry.
- Oregonians may not eat ice cream on Sundays.
- Canned corn may not be used as bait when fishing.
- One may not bathe without wearing suitable clothing.
- In Marion County, ministers are forbidden to eat onions or garlic before giving a sermon.
- In Hood River, it is illegal to juggle without a license.

MINI-BIO

WAYNE MORSE: MAVERICK SENATOR

When he won a seat in the U.S. Senate in 1944, Oregon's Wayne Morse (1900–1974) ran as a Republican. In 1952, he left the Republican Party and became a Democrat. Morse's move earned him the nickname the Maverick Senator. (A maverick is a stray cow that wanders on the range.) Like a maverick of the West, he wasn't owned by anyone. He was often outspoken about government policies, including the Vietnam War. He served in the Senate until 1969.

? **Want to know more?** See bioguide.congress. gov/scripts/biodisplay.pl?index=m001014

THE LEGISLATIVE BRANCH

Richard Chambers loved the outdoors. He dreamed of climbing every mountain in Oregon. Yet wherever he went, he was dismayed to see empty cans and bottles that people thoughtlessly tossed along the roads. In the summer of 1968, Chambers urged his state representative to support recycling through a bill that would make disposable cans and bottles illegal in Oregon. In 1971, after much hard work by Chambers and many others, Oregon passed the Bottle Bill, requiring cans and bottles in the state to be returnable. Customers collect a deposit when they return bottles and cans to the store, and at the same time they help keep the state clean and beautiful. The Bottle Bill is just one example of how an Oregon citizen helped pass a law that makes life better for the state's people. The state led the nation with this initiative.

The legislature, officially called the Legislative Assembly, is divided into two houses, which meet in the four-story capitol. The upper house, or senate, has 30 members. State senators are elected to four-year terms. The lower house, or house of representatives, has 60 members who are elected to two-year terms. The assembly meets in odd-numbered years. Sessions begin on the second Monday in January and run until the assembly's work is done.

THE EXECUTIVE BRANCH

A number of elected officials serve in Oregon's executive branch. They advise the governor and carry out specific tasks. These officials include the secretary of state, attorney general, treasurer, and superintendent of public instruction. Oregon's chief executive, the governor, is elected to a four-year term. Unlike many other states, Oregon does not have a lieutenant governor. If the governor cannot continue in office, the secretary of state takes over his or her duties.

The governor has many responsibilities, including creating a budget for the state government. He or she serves as commander of the state military and can call out forces to help in an emergency. The governor also signs bills into law or has the power to veto, or turn down, a bill. Each year, the governor delivers a speech called the State of the State address. In that speech, the governor outlines current conditions in the state and offers recommendations for improvements.

SEE IT HERE!

MAHONIA HALL

The official residence of Oregon's governor is a lovely mansion called Mahonia Hall. The state purchased Mahonia Hall in 1988. Until that time, the state rented houses for its governors. Built in 1924, Mahonia Hall has a magnificent third-floor ballroom and a built-in pipe organ. Formal gardens that are open to the public surround it.

MINI-BIO

MARK HATFIELD: SPEAKING HIS MIND

Mark Hatfield (1922–) was elected to the legislative assembly in 1950, and in 1956 became the youngest secretary of state in Oregon history. He served two terms as governor (1959–1967) before he stepped onto the national scene. He served in the U.S. Senate from 1967 to 1997. During the 1960s, he took a strong stand against the Vietnam War and called for a freeze on developing nuclear weapons. At the same time, he supported the farming and logging industries. Throughout his long career in politics, Hatfield never lost an election.

? **Want to know more?** See bioguide.congress. gov/scripts/biodisplay.pl?index=H000343

MINI-BIO

HERBERT HOOVER: OREGON'S PRESIDENT

Herbert Hoover (1874–1964) was born in Iowa but moved to Oregon to live with an uncle after his parents died. He lived in Newberg until 1891, when he entered Stanford University in California. During and after World War I, Hoover led the effort to feed the starving people of Europe. In 1928, he was elected president of the United States. He was in office when the Great Depression began, and many Americans harshly criticized him for failing to pull the country out of the crisis.

? Want to know more? See http://millercenter.virginia.edu/academic/americanpresident/hoover

WORDS TO KNOW

malpractice *poor treatment that harms a patient*

appealed *asked a court to change the decision of a lower court*

Representing Oregon

This list shows the number of elected officials who represent Oregon, both on the state and national levels.

OFFICE	NUMBER	LENGTH OF TERM
State senators	30	4 years
State representatives	60	2 years
U.S. senators	2	6 years
U.S. representatives	5	2 years
Presidential electors	7	—

THE JUDICIAL BRANCH

Oregon is divided into various circuit court districts. Judges in circuit courts rule on local civil cases, such as divorce and medical **malpractice**. They also handle criminal cases ranging from shoplifting to murder. Cases can be **appealed** from the circuit courts to the court of appeals and, finally, to the supreme court in Salem. The supreme court, the highest court in the state, has seven judges. Each judge is elected to serve a six-year term.

LOCAL GOVERNMENT

Oregon has 36 counties and about 240 cities and towns. Towns and cities select their own form of government. Most small towns have a mayor and a town council. Most large cities have a form of government called council-manager. The city of Portland has an unusual

Oregon Counties

This map shows the 36 counties in Oregon. Salem, the state capital, is indicated with a star.

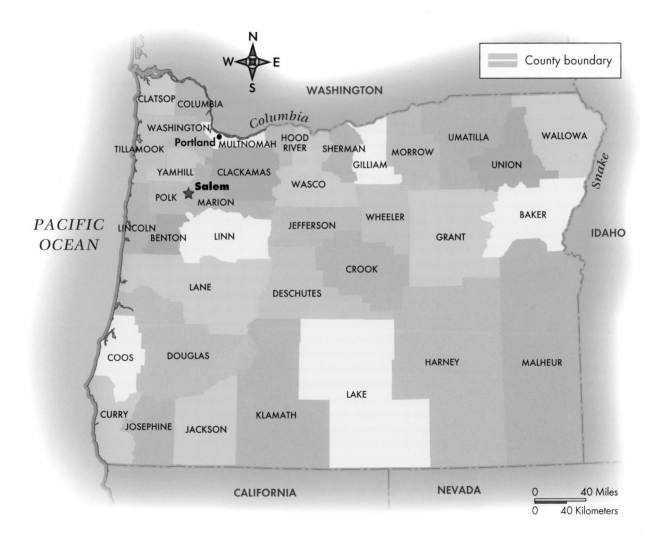

form of government found nowhere else in the state. It is governed by a mayor and four officials called commissioners. These leaders help the mayor by managing various public programs.

State Flag

The state flag has a field of navy blue with the state seal in gold, which appears above the year in which Oregon became a state, 1859. The flag was officially adopted in 1925. The reverse side of the flag shows a beaver, the state animal. Oregon has the only state flag with an image on the back.

State Seal

The state seal is a shield with a bald eagle above it. Below the shield are 33 stars—signifying that Oregon was the 33rd state admitted to the Union—and a ribbon carrying the inscription "The Union." Above the ribbon are scenes that represent Oregon history. The mountains and forests of Oregon against the sun setting over the Pacific Ocean provide a background for an ox-drawn wagon, an elk, a departing British warship, and an arriving American merchant ship. Below the ribbon, a sheaf of wheat, a plow, and a miner's pick symbolize Oregon's resources and industries.

READ ABOUT

Chefs put the finishing touches on a crab and truffle dish at the Oregon Truffle Festival in Eugene.

CHAPTER EIGHT

ECONOMY

★

A FARMER DRIVES A TRACTOR OVER A FIELD NEAR PENDLETON. A chef prepares a meal in a health-food restaurant in Eugene. A clerk sells a pair of running shoes in a Beaverton store. In Portland, dockworkers load a containership bound for China. All of these people are contributing to Oregon's economy.

DOING THINGS FOR OTHERS

Service industries are industries in which people are paid to do things for others. A guide leading a group of mountain climbers up Mount Hood, a server in a Eugene restaurant delivering lunch to customers, and a Portland real estate agent taking a client to look at a new house all work in service industries. Service industries account for about three-fourths of Oregon's **gross state product**. Finance, insurance, and real estate make up the largest segment of the state's service industries. These industries are chiefly centered in the Portland area.

The service industries known as community, business, and personal services employ more people than any other segment of the economy. This group of service industries includes private lawyers and doctors, hairdressers, auto repair people, and electricians. Other important service industries include hospitality (restaurants and hotels) and wholesale and retail trade.

The state and federal governments employ thousands of service-industry workers in Oregon. Government employees include public school teach-

WORD TO KNOW

gross state product *the total value of all the goods and services produced in a state*

Construction workers are part of Oregon's service industry.

ers, foresters, and workers in public hospitals. People who work at state colleges and universities are also government employees.

MAKING THINGS

Decades ago, people in Oregon relied on timber to keep the economy strong. But these days, business in Oregon is more focused on other industries.

In 1964, University of Oregon coach Bill Bowerman and a university track star named Phil Knight started a small company that sold shoes for athletes. The company expanded, and in 1971 it became Nike Footwear. Today, Nike, Inc., based in Beaverton, produces sportswear for people around the world. Nike is in keeping with Oregonians' tradition of athletic excellence and their love of the outdoors.

The high-technology industries are well established in Oregon. Two major computer manufacturers—Intel and Hewlett-Packard—have branches in the state. Oregon is also a leading producer of digital television sets.

Oregon's timber industry has given rise to the production of lumber and other wood-related products. Plants also turn out plywood, particleboard, and wood veneer. Machine shops in Oregon assemble equipment used in the wood-processing industries.

DOUGLAS ENGELBART: "FATHER OF THE INTERNET"

From the time he was a student at Oregon State University, Douglas Engelbart (1925–) dreamed of using technology to extend the reach of the human mind. He studied electrical engineering and quickly moved into the brand-new field of computer technology. In the 1960s, he pioneered a very early version of communication between computers using telephone lines. This online communication evolved into the Internet. Engelbart also invented a device for moving the cursor on a computer screen—the mouse.

? Want to know more? See www.ibiblio.org/pioneers/engelbart.html

SEE IT HERE!

A. C. GILBERT DISCOVERY VILLAGE

A. C. Gilbert of Salem believed that playing and learning went hand in hand. In 1913, he invented the Erector Set, a toy that has since taught millions of children about construction and engineering. You can explore many of Gilbert's 150 inventions at the A. C. Gilbert Discovery Village in Salem.

Major Agricultural and Mining Products

This map shows where Oregon's major agricultural and mining products come from. See a milk carton? That means dairy is found there.

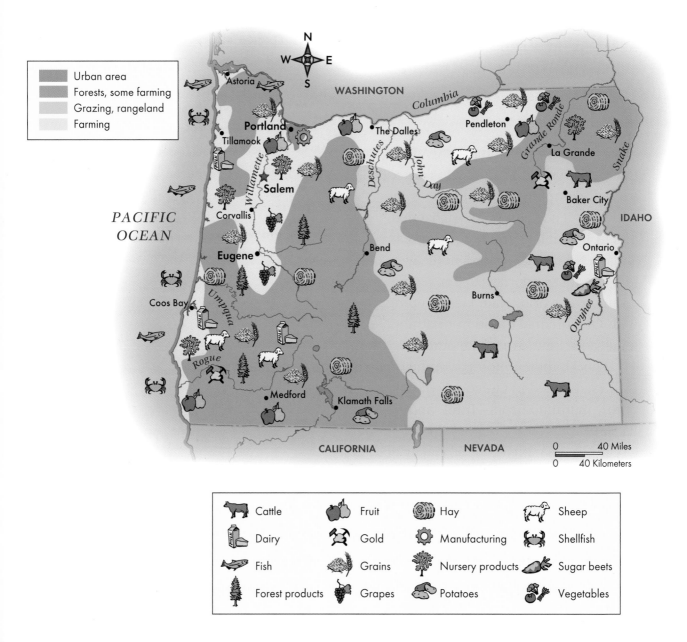

Map Legend:
- Urban area
- Forests, some farming
- Grazing, rangeland
- Farming

Symbols:
- Cattle
- Dairy
- Fish
- Forest products
- Fruit
- Gold
- Grains
- Grapes
- Hay
- Manufacturing
- Nursery products
- Potatoes
- Sheep
- Shellfish
- Sugar beets
- Vegetables

A cowgirl driving cattle near the Cascades

FROM LAND AND SEA

About 30 percent of Oregon's land is devoted to farming. Cattle and sheep graze on the high plateau east of the Cascades. Farmers in this region also grow wheat and potatoes. Western Oregon has many farms as well. The Willamette Valley

Top Products

Agriculture Bulbs and other nursery products, timber, hazelnuts, beef, wool, dairy products, poultry, wheat, potatoes

Manufacturing Electronic equipment, lumber and wood products, processed foods, fabricated metal products, paper products

Minerals Sand and gravel, clays, lime, pumice, emery

Fishing Crabs, shrimp, salmon, tuna

A tulip farm in the Willamette Valley

About 99 percent of the hazelnuts grown in the United States come from the Willamette Valley.

is a leading producer of flowers and flower bulbs. Tulip, daffodil, narcissus, lily, and other bulbs from Oregon are shipped to gardeners all over the world.

Oregon is the nation's only major source of hazelnuts, or filberts. In 2004, 37,500 tons of hazelnuts were harvested from Oregon farms.

Nearly half of Oregon is covered with forests. Oregon is one of the nation's leading timber producers. Douglas fir, which grows west of the Cascades, is the state's chief timber export. Ponderosa pine, white pine, and lodgepole pine are logged in eastern Oregon.

Sand and gravel for the construction industry are mined in most parts of Oregon. Oregon also contains deposits of clay, lime, and pumice. It is the only state to produce emery.

Fish was once the staple food in Oregon. Today, the fishing industry is still an important part of Oregon's economy. Crabs, shrimp, and salmon are harvested and sold commercially.

FAQ

Q8 WHAT IS EMERY?

A8 Emery is a black or dark gray mineral used for grinding and polishing. It is used in the manufacture of emery boards for filing fingernails and in the production of asphalt.

What Do Oregonians Do?

This color-coded chart shows what industries Oregonians work in.

19.1% Educational services, health care, and social assistance, 328,866

13.3% Manufacturing, 227,582

12.7% Retail trade, 217,715

9.6% Professional, scientific, management, administrative, and waste management services, 164,932

8.6% Arts, entertainment, recreation, accommodation, and food services, 148,150

7.7% Construction, 131,231

6.7% Finance, insurance, real estate, rental, and leasing, 114,054

4.6% Other services, except public administration, 78,242

4.5% Public administration, 77,731

4.3% Transportation, warehousing, and utilities, 73,147

3.7% Wholesale trade, 62,600

3.1% Agriculture, forestry, fishing, hunting, and mining, 53,160

2.1% Information, 35,716

Source: U.S. Census Bureau, 2000

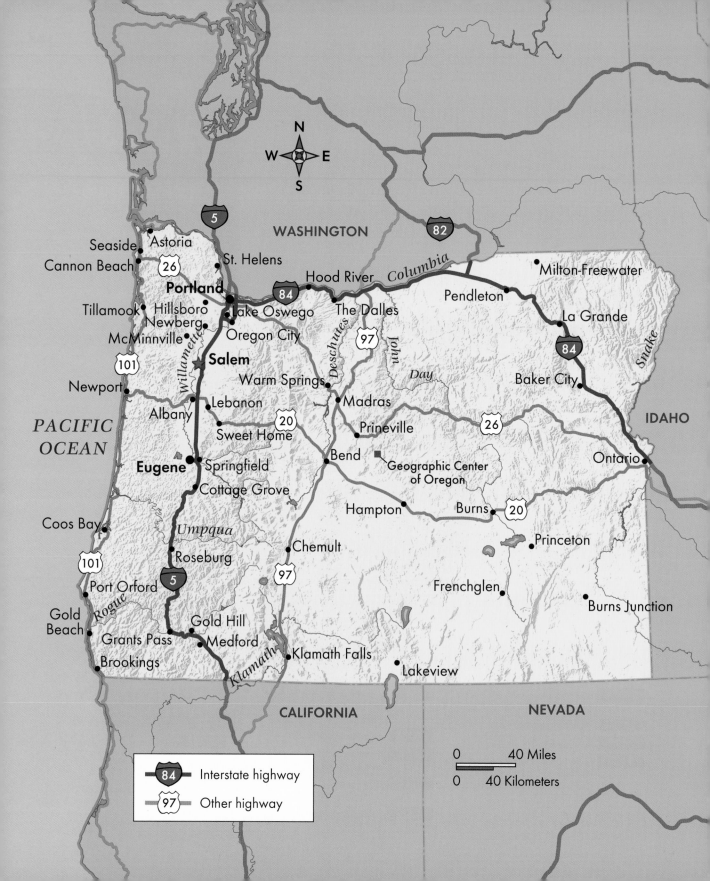

CHAPTER NINE

TRAVEL GUIDE

★

FROM THE CRASHING WAVES OF
THE PACIFIC COAST TO THE SNOW-
CAPPED CASCADES, OREGON IS A
LAND OF STUNNING NATURAL BEAUTY. Visit
the state's beaches, hike its trails, observe its
wildlife, and walk in the footsteps of people
who lived long ago. And be sure to check out
the museums listed on page 131 for even
more cool stuff to see!

← Follow along with this map. We'll begin in Seaside and
travel all the way to Ontario.

THE NORTHERN COAST

THINGS TO DO: Imagine camping with Lewis and Clark, taste local cheeses in Tillamook, or check out one of the world's tallest sea stacks.

Seaside

★ **Lewis and Clark Campsite:** Seaside is considered the official end of the Lewis and Clark Trail. The expedition's campsite has been reconstructed based on Clark's journals and sketches.

Cannon Beach

★ **Haystack Rock:** The tallest of Oregon's many sea stacks, Haystack Rock stands 235 feet (72 m) above the beach at low tide. Thousands of seabirds nest on it.

Haystack Rock

Astoria

★ **Fort Clatsop:** This was the winter encampment for the Corps of Discovery from December 1805 to March 1806. Visitors can tour the fort and an interpretive center—as well as hike some of the trails.

Tillamook

★ **Tillamook Cheese Visitor's Center:** Sample a variety of local cheeses at the edge of prime dairy country.

★ **Tillamook Forest Center:** This conservation center at the heart of the Tillamook Burn—an area ravaged by a series of wildfires in the 1930s and 1940s—tells the story of the natural disaster and how it changed forest management practices.

★ **Tillamook Air Museum:** Visitors can see more than 30 aircraft, all housed in a wooden World War II blimp hangar.

Haystack Rock is the third-tallest sea stack in the world!

Jellyfish at the Oregon Coast Aquarium

Newport

★ **Oregon Coast Aquarium:** See
190 species of birds, fish, and sea
mammals at this aquarium, which
sprawls over 29 acres (12 hect-
ares). Seals, sea otters, and giant
octopuses swim in their natural
habitat. The aquarium includes
the largest seabird **aviary** in North
America.

★ **Yaquina Head Lighthouse:**
Standing 93 feet (28 m) high, this
lighthouse tower is the tallest on
the Oregon coast. Climb to the top
for a magnificent view of beaches,
rocks, and waves.

Yaquina Head Lighthouse

SOUTHERN COAST

THINGS TO DO: Watch
towering waves at Shore
Acres State Park, see fishing boats hoisted
ashore at Port Orford, or explore Oregon's last
working lighthouse.

Coos Bay

★ **Shore Acres State Park:** From a
cliff-top shelter, look out to sea and
watch for whales. Waves crash into
the cliffs, sending jets of foam 50
feet (15 m) into the air.

Port Orford

★ **Port Orford** is a fishing center
with no natural harbor. Each morning, the fishing boats are lowered
into the water; each night, they are
swung up and out on huge wooden
booms.

Gold Beach

★ **Cape Blanco Lighthouse** is
the last working lighthouse on
Oregon's coast.

WORD TO KNOW

aviary *a large walk-in enclosure
where birds are allowed to fly freely*

SOUTH-WESTERN OREGON

THINGS TO DO: Climb Lower Table Rock at Medford or challenge the force of gravity at the Oregon House of Mystery in Gold Hill.

Gold Hill

★ **Oregon House of Mystery:** Located in a strange area known as the Oregon Vortex, this museum challenges assumptions about gravity and perception. Balls seem to roll uphill, poles balance on end, and people appear to shrink or grow before your eyes.

Medford

★ **Lower Table Rock:** Take in a wonderful view of the Rogue River and the Siskiyou Mountains from the flat top of this giant rock. Upper Table Rock, nearby, is higher and more difficult to climb.

Lower Table Rock

The waterslide at Willamalane Park

WILLAMETTE VALLEY

THINGS TO DO: See how paper is made, glide down a giant waterslide, or visit Herbert Hoover's boyhood home.

Springfield

★ **Weyerhaeuser Containerboard Factory:** Tour this working paper mill and see how wood pulp is turned into giant rolls of paper. To visit the factory, you'll have to put in earplugs and wear a hard hat.

★ **Willamalane Park and Recreation District:** This park features the only wave-action pool in the Northwest and a giant waterslide you won't forget!

Newberg

★ **Hoover-Minthorn House:** Herbert Hoover, the 31st U.S. president, lived here with his aunt and uncle when he was a teenager. Many pieces of the family's furniture are on display. Young Herbert used to pick and eat pears from a tree that still grows and bears fruit on the grounds of the house.

McMinnville

★ **Evergeen Aviation & Space Museum:** This museum is home to the *Spruce Goose*, Howard Hughes's World War II "flying boat," and it features artifacts and information about the history of aviation.

The *Spruce Goose* at the Evergreen Aviation & Space Museum

Albany

★ **Monteith House:** Pioneers Walter and Thomas Monteith built this house in 1849. Over the years, the house served as a church, meetinghouse, and military headquarters. It has been restored to look much as it did in the 1850s.

PORTLAND AREA

THINGS TO DO: Ride a trolley, stop and smell some roses, say hello to an elephant, or try on some hockey gear.

Lake Oswego

★ **Willamette Shore Trolley** runs from Lake Oswego to Portland along the west bank of the Willamette River. The ride offers lovely river views, but be prepared to clatter through one of Oregon's darkest tunnels as well.

Portland

★ **World Forestry Center:** Forests have always been important to Oregonians, both for logging and recreation. The center enhances our understanding of forests to ensure their preservation for the future.

The rose garden at Washington Park

★ **Washington Park:** This lovely park in Portland's West Hills features a 5-acre (2 ha) Japanese garden that features flowers, shrubs, and cherry trees. The park zoo has many species of animals native to the Northwest, in addition to an exhibit of Asian elephants.

★ **Oregon Sports Hall of Fame and Museum:** This hall honors Oregon athletes and celebrates a wide array of team and individual sports. A nonstop giant-screen video shows the 100 greatest moments of Oregon sports history. In one exhibit, called the Locker Room, visitors can get hands-on experience with bats, balls, and gear.

★ **Oregon Historical Society:** The society's museum features exhibits about Oregon art, World War II, and other aspects of the state's history.

★ **International Rose Test Garden:** Portland is sometimes called the Rose City, and this magnificent park helps explain why. In spring and summer, it is alive with color and fragrance as some 400 varieties of roses burst into bloom.

★ **Oregon Museum of Science and Industry:** Visitors will find five exhibit halls, eight science labs, a big-screen OMNIMAX theater, and a planetarium. Learn about science by touching a volcano, experiencing an earthquake, or uncovering a fossil!

Innovation Station at the Oregon Museum of Science and Industry

HENRY LEWIS PITTOCK: THE MAN BEHIND THE OREGONIAN

When he was 17, Henry Lewis Pittock (1836–1919) left Pittsburgh and set out for Oregon. According to some stories, he made the entire journey barefoot! He arrived nearly penniless and took a job as a printer with a weekly paper called the Oregonian. Room and board were his only wages. Pittock was a hard worker and clever businessman, and he took over the paper when the owner left in 1861. He built the Oregonian into the state's leading daily newspaper. He also established a thriving paper mill, which spurred Oregon's papermaking industry.

? Want to know more? See www.pittockmansion.org/historians.asp

★ **Pittock Mansion:** Built in 1909 by publisher Henry Pittock, this mansion has 22 rooms that have been restored to look as they did early in the 20th century. From the grounds, you can see a breathtaking view of downtown Portland and the mountains to the east.

Oregon City

★ **McLoughlin House:** Although it has been moved from its original location, this house looks much as it did when Dr. John McLoughlin lived here in 1846. Furniture, paintings, and documents tell the story of the man remembered as the Father of Oregon.

★ **End of the Oregon Trail Interpretive Center:** Exhibits and hands-on activities help visitors imagine what travelers on the Oregon Trail experienced.

NORTH CENTRAL OREGON

THINGS TO DO: Try to solve a whodunit on a dinner-theater train or admire Mount Hood from a railcar.

Prineville

★ **Crooked River Railroad Dinner Train:** This special train runs 38 miles (61 km) from Redmond to Prineville. Passengers become part of a theatrical production in which a murder is enacted, and everyone aboard tries to unravel the mystery.

★ **Sorosis Park:** This 15-acre (6 ha) park on the cliffs offers a splendid view of the city and the Columbia River Gorge. Missionaries once preached from the park's Sermon Rock.

Bend

★ **High Desert Museum:** This facility celebrates the wildlife, culture, art, and natural resources of the High Desert region.

Hood River

★ **Mount Hood Railroad:** A ride on the scenic railroad is a wonderful way to enjoy spectacular views of Mount Hood and the Columbia River Gorge. The train is pulled by a diesel engine built in 1910.

Mount Hood Railroad

Warm Springs

★ **Museum at Warm Springs:** Located on the Warm Springs Indian Reservation, this museum offers exhibits and educational programs about Native American heritage. See how early peoples lived and what clothing they wore.

EASTERN OREGON

THINGS TO DO: Wander through a gold-rush ghost town, learn about the Oregon Trail from a unique perspective, or hike Steens Mountain for a spectacular view.

Baker City

★ **Auburn ghost town:** On October 23, 1863, a prospector named Henry Griffen discovered gold in Auburn, and in six months it became a booming gold-rush town of 6,000 people. The gold didn't last, and by 1867 Auburn was a ghost town. Wander through the crumbled remains of houses and stores, and try to imagine the eager miners who once made Auburn their home.

La Grande

★ **Ladd Marsh Wildlife Area:** This once-threatened wetland has been carefully restored and is now alive with herons, ducks, and other waterfowl. Bring your wading boots and binoculars, and see how many species you can spot!

Pendleton

★ **Tamástslikt Cultural Institute:** The institute presents the history and achievements of the Cayuses, Walla Wallas, and Umatillas of eastern Oregon. The story of the Indians is told in three sections: "We Were," "We Are," and "We Will Be." Find out what Native Americans thought about the Oregon Trail.

Steens Mountain

Frenchglen

★ **Steens Mountain:** This mountain has a variety of trails for both beginning and more experienced climbers to enjoy. The view from the peak is well worth the effort!

Ontario

★ **Four Rivers Cultural Center:** This museum traces the many cultures that have merged in Oregon's Treasure Valley. Displays tell the stories of the Northern Paiutes, Japanese Americans, Latinos, and European Americans who made the region their home.

An exhibit at the Tamástslikt Cultural Institute

WRITING PROJECTS

Check out these ideas for creating campaign brochures and writing you-are-there editorials. Or research famous Oregonians.

118

ART PROJECTS

Create a great PowerPoint presentation, illustrate the state song, or learn about the state quarter and design your own.

119

OREGON 1859
CRATER LAKE
2005
E PLURIBUS UNUM

TIMELINE

What happened when? This timeline highlights important events in the state's history—and shows what was happening throughout the United States at the same time.

122

FAST FACTS

Use this section to find fascinating facts about state symbols, land area and population statistics, weather, sports teams, and much more.

126

GLOSSARY

Remember the Words to Know from the chapters in this book? They're all collected here.

125

SCIENCE, TECHNOLOGY, & MATH PROJECTS

Make weather maps, graph population statistics, and research endangered species that live in the state.

120

PRIMARY VS. SECONDARY SOURCES

121

So what are primary and secondary sources? And what's the diff? This section explains all that and where you can find them.

BIOGRAPHICAL DICTIONARY

133

This at-a-glance guide highlights some of the state's most important and influential people. Visit this section and read about their contributions to the state, the country, and the world.

RESOURCES

Books, Web sites, DVDs, and more. Take a look at these additional sources for information about the state.

137

WRITING PROJECTS

★ ★ ★

Write a Memoir, Journal, or Editorial for Your School Newspaper!
Picture Yourself . . .

★ fishing the rivers along Oregon's coast in the 1790s. Where would you fish, and what tools would you use? How would you dry and store the fish you catch?

   SEE: Chapter Two, pages 22–30.

★ on the Oregon Trail. You are with your family, traveling hundreds of miles with no end in sight. What would your responsibilities be?

   SEE: Chapter Three, pages 44–46.

Create an Election Brochure or Web Site!

Run for office! Throughout this book, you've read about some issues that concern Oregon today. As a candidate for governor of Oregon, create a campaign brochure or Web site.

★ Explain how you meet the qualifications to be governor of Oregon.

★ Talk about the three or four major issues you'll focus on if you're elected.

★ Remember, you'll be responsible for Oregon's budget. How would you spend the taxpayers' money?

   SEE: Chapter Seven, pages 91–94.

   GO TO: Oregon's government Web site at www. oregon.gov. You might also want to read some local newspapers that are available online.

Create an Interview Script with a Person from Oregon!

★ Research various Oregonians, such as Mel Blanc, Beverly Cleary, Matt Groening, Mary Decker Slaney, or Phil Knight.

★ Based on your research, pick one person you would most like to talk with.

★ Write a script of the interview. What questions would you ask? How would this person answer? Create a question-and-answer format. You may want to supplement this writing project with a voice-recording dramatization of the interview.

   SEE: Chapters Five, Six, and Seven, pages 62–95, and the Biographical Dictionary, pages 133–136.

   GO TO: Sites such as bluebook.state.or.us/ notable/nothome.htm

Nike CEO Phil Knight

ART PROJECTS

★ ★ ★

Create a PowerPoint Presentation or Visitors' Guide
Welcome to Oregon!

Oregon's a great place to visit and to live! From its natural beauty to its bustling cities and historical sites, there's plenty to see and do. In your PowerPoint presentation or brochure, highlight 10 to 15 of Oregon's amazing landmarks. Be sure to include:

★ a map of the state showing where these sites are located

★ photos, illustrations, Web links, natural history facts, geographic stats, climate and weather, plants and wildlife, and recent discoveries

SEE: Chapter Nine, pages 106–115.

GO TO: The official tourism Web site for Oregon at www.traveloregon.com. Download and print maps, photos, and vacation ideas for tourists.

Illustrate the Lyrics to the Oregon State Song
("Oregon, My Oregon")

Use markers, paints, photos, collages, colored pencils, or computer graphics to illustrate the lyrics to "Oregon, My Oregon." Turn your illustrations into a picture book, or scan them into PowerPoint and add music.

SEE: The lyrics to "Oregon, My Oregon" on page 128.

GO TO: The Oregon state Web site at www. oregon.gov to find out more about the origin of the Oregon state song "Oregon, My Oregon."

Research Oregon's State Quarter

From 1999 to 2008, the U.S. Mint introduced new quarters commemorating each of the 50 states in the order that they were admitted to the Union. Each state's quarter features a unique design on its back, or reverse.

GO TO: www.usmint.gov/kids and find out what's featured on the back of the Oregon quarter.

Research and write an essay explaining:

★ the significance of each image

★ who designed the quarter

★ who chose the final design

Design your own Oregon state quarter. What images would you choose for the reverse?

Make a poster showing the Oregon quarter and label each image.

SCIENCE, TECHNOLOGY, & MATH PROJECTS

★ ★ ★

Graph Population Statistics!

★ Compare population statistics (such as ethnic background, birth, death, and literacy rates) in Oregon counties or major cities.

★ On your graph or chart, look at population density and write sentences describing what the population statistics show; graph one set of population statistics and write a paragraph explaining what the graphs reveal.

SEE: Chapter Six, pages 76–77.

GO TO: The official Web site for the U.S. Census Bureau at www.census.gov and at http://quickfacts.census.gov/qfd/states/41000.html to find out more about population statistics, how they work, and what the statistics are for Oregon.

Create a Weather Map of Oregon!

Use your knowledge of Oregon's geography to research and identify conditions that result in specific weather events. What is it about the geography of Oregon that makes it vulnerable to things such as thunderstorms and heavy rainfall? Create a weather map or poster that shows the weather patterns across the state. Include a caption explaining the technology used to measure weather phenomena and provide data.

SEE: Chapter One, pages 8–21.

GO TO: The National Oceanic and Atmospheric Administration's National Weather Service Web site at www.weather.gov for weather maps and forecasts for Oregon.

Northern spotted owl

Track Endangered Species

Using your knowledge of Oregon's wildlife, research which animals and plants are endangered or threatened.

★ Find out what the state is doing to protect these species.

★ Chart known populations of the animals and plants, and report on changes in certain geographic areas.

SEE: Chapter One, pages 17–21.

GO TO: Web sites such as www.endangeredspecie.com/states/or.htm or www.dfw.state.or.us/LIP/2004_t&e_books.pdf for lists of endangered species in Oregon.

PRIMARY VS. SECONDARY SOURCES

★ ★ ★

What's the Diff?

Your teacher may require at least one or two primary sources and one or two secondary sources for your assignment. So, what's the difference between the two?

★ **Primary sources are original.** You are reading the actual words of someone's diary, journal, letter, autobiography, or interview. Primary sources can also be photographs, maps, prints, cartoons, news/film footage, posters, first-person newspaper articles, drawings, musical scores, and recordings. By the way, when you conduct a survey, interview someone, shoot a video, or take photographs to include in a project, you are creating primary sources!

★ **Secondary sources are what you find in encyclopedias, textbooks, articles, biographies, and almanacs.** These are written by a person or group of people who tell about something that happened to someone else. Secondary sources also recount what another person said or did. This book is an example of a secondary source.

Now that you know what primary sources are—where can you find them?

★ **Your school or local library:** Check the library catalog for collections of original writings, government documents, musical scores, and so on. Some of this material may be stored on microfilm. The Library of Congress Web site (www.loc.gov) is an excellent online resource for primary source materials.

★ **Historical societies:** These organizations keep historical documents, photographs, and other materials. Staff members can help you find what you are looking for. History museums are also great places to see primary sources firsthand.

★ **The Internet:** There are lots of sites that have primary sources you can download and use in a project or assignment.

TIMELINE

★ ★ ★

U.S. Events `1500` **Oregon Events**

1543
A Spanish ship sails up the Pacific coast to what is now southern Oregon.

1565
Spanish admiral Pedro Menéndez de Avilés founds St. Augustine, Florida, the oldest continuously occupied European settlement in the continental United States.

1577
Sir Francis Drake sails to the coast of Oregon and claims the land for England.

`1600`

1607
The first permanent English settlement in North America is established at Jamestown.

A Nez Perce man on horseback

1619
The first African indentured laborers in English North America are purchased for work in the Jamestown settlement.

1620
Pilgrims found Plymouth Colony, the second permanent English settlement.

1682
René-Robert Cavelier, Sieur de La Salle, claims more than 1 million square miles (2.6 million sq km) of territory in the Mississippi River basin for France, naming it Louisiana.

`1700`

1720s
Horses reach the Columbia Plateau and change life for the Native people there.

1754–63
England and France fight over North American colonial lands in the French and Indian War. By the end of the war, France has ceded all of its land west of the Mississippi to Spain and its Canadian territories to England.

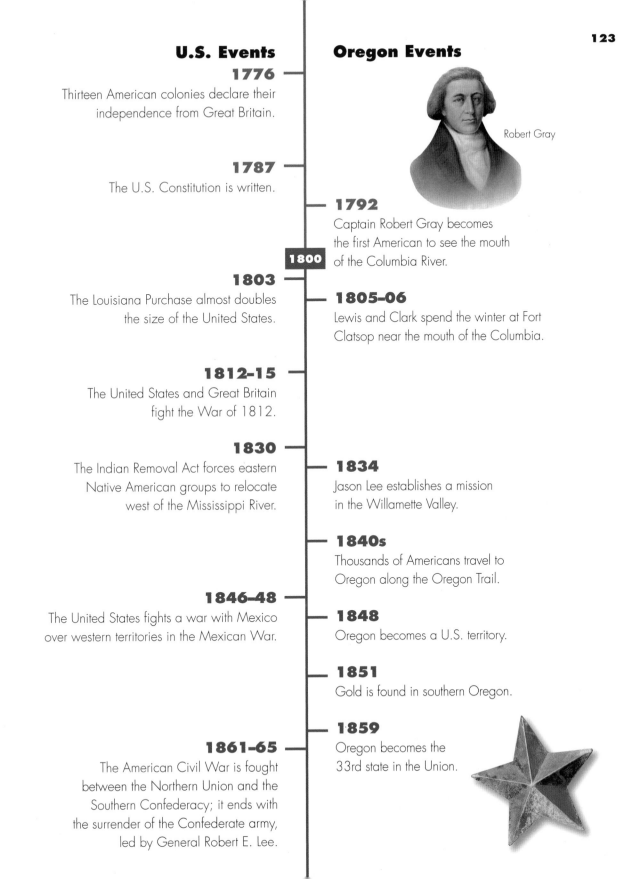

U.S. Events **Oregon Events**

1776
Thirteen American colonies declare their independence from Great Britain.

Robert Gray

1787
The U.S. Constitution is written.

1792
Captain Robert Gray becomes the first American to see the mouth of the Columbia River.

1800

1803
The Louisiana Purchase almost doubles the size of the United States.

1805–06
Lewis and Clark spend the winter at Fort Clatsop near the mouth of the Columbia.

1812–15
The United States and Great Britain fight the War of 1812.

1830
The Indian Removal Act forces eastern Native American groups to relocate west of the Mississippi River.

1834
Jason Lee establishes a mission in the Willamette Valley.

1840s
Thousands of Americans travel to Oregon along the Oregon Trail.

1846–48
The United States fights a war with Mexico over western territories in the Mexican War.

1848
Oregon becomes a U.S. territory.

1851
Gold is found in southern Oregon.

1859
Oregon becomes the 33rd state in the Union.

1861–65
The American Civil War is fought between the Northern Union and the Southern Confederacy; it ends with the surrender of the Confederate army, led by General Robert E. Lee.

U.S. Events

Oregon Events

1877
The Wallowa band of Nez Perces refuses to move to a reservation and leads the U.S. Army on a four-month chase.

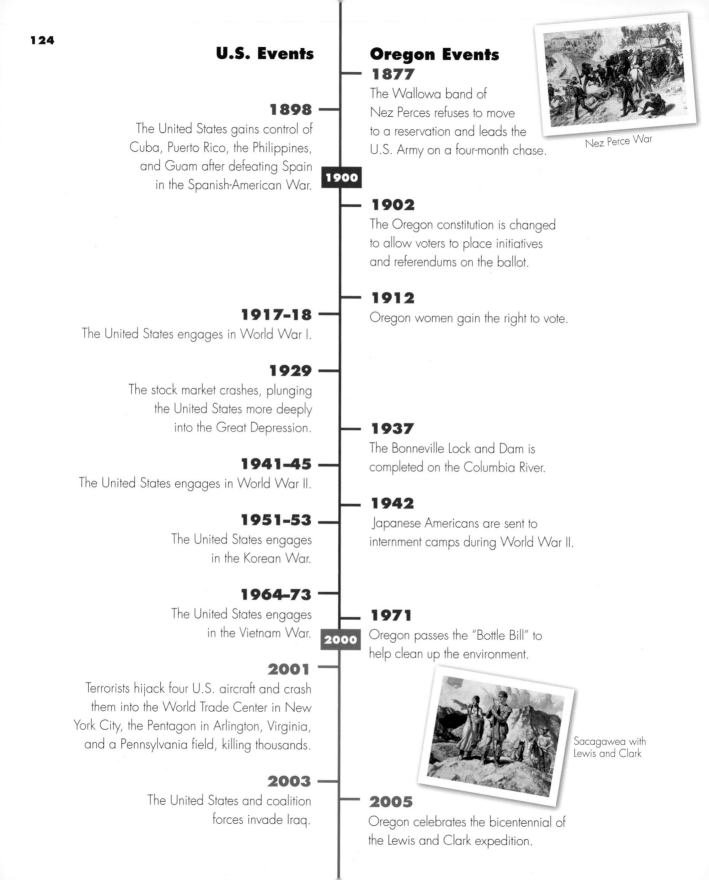

Nez Perce War

1898
The United States gains control of Cuba, Puerto Rico, the Philippines, and Guam after defeating Spain in the Spanish-American War.

1900

1902
The Oregon constitution is changed to allow voters to place initiatives and referendums on the ballot.

1912
Oregon women gain the right to vote.

1917–18
The United States engages in World War I.

1929
The stock market crashes, plunging the United States more deeply into the Great Depression.

1937
The Bonneville Lock and Dam is completed on the Columbia River.

1941–45
The United States engages in World War II.

1942
Japanese Americans are sent to internment camps during World War II.

1951–53
The United States engages in the Korean War.

1964–73
The United States engages in the Vietnam War.

2000

1971
Oregon passes the "Bottle Bill" to help clean up the environment.

2001
Terrorists hijack four U.S. aircraft and crash them into the World Trade Center in New York City, the Pentagon in Arlington, Virginia, and a Pennsylvania field, killing thousands.

Sacagawea with Lewis and Clark

2003
The United States and coalition forces invade Iraq.

2005
Oregon celebrates the bicentennial of the Lewis and Clark expedition.

GLOSSARY

★ ★ ★

amendment a change to a law or legal document

appealed asked a court to change the decision of a lower court

archaeologists people who study the remains of past human societies

aviary a large walk-in enclosure where birds are allowed to fly freely

breechcloths garments worn by men over their lower bodies

emigrants people who leave their homes to live in another land

glaciers slow-moving masses of ice

gross state product the total value of all the goods and services produced in a state

hydroelectric power electricity generated by the force of water passing over a dam

immunity natural protection against disease

internment camps places where people are confined, usually during wartime

malpractice poor treatment that harms a patient

missionaries people who try to convert others to a religion

missions places created by a religious group to spread its beliefs

obsidian jet-black volcanic glass

pemmican dried salmon or other meat

plateau an elevated part of the earth with steep slopes

quadriplegic totally or partially paralyzed from the neck down

recall to remove elected officials from office

reservations lands set aside for Native Americans to live on

segregated separated from others according to race, class, ethnic group, religion, or other factors

suffrage the right to vote

symmetry balance, evenness on both sides

taboos rules about how activities such as hunting and preparing food must be performed

transcontinental crossing an entire continent

tributary a river that flows into a larger river

FAST FACTS

★ ★ ★

State Symbols

Statehood date	February 14, 1859, 33rd state
Origin of state name	Unknown, but one theory holds that the name may have come from the French word *ouragan*, meaning "hurricane"
State capital	Salem
State nickname	The Beaver State
State motto	"She flies with her own wings"
State bird	Western meadowlark
State flower	Oregon grape
State fish	Chinook salmon
State mammal	Beaver
State insect	Oregon swallowtail
State nut	Hazelnut
State song	"Oregon, My Oregon"
State tree	Douglas fir
State shell	Oregon hairy triton
State gemstone	Oregon sunstone
State rock	Thunderegg
State fair	Late August–early September at Salem

State seal

Geography

Total area; rank	98,381 square miles (254,807 sq km); 9th
Land; rank	95,997 square miles (248,632 sq km); 10th
Water; rank	2,384 square miles (6,175 sq km); 19th
Inland water; rank	1,050 square miles (2,719 sq km); 19th
Coastal water; rank	80 square miles (207 sq km); 17th
Territorial water; rank	1,254 square miles (3,248 sq km); 9th
Geographic center	Crook, 25 miles (40 km) south-southeast of Prineville
Latitude	42° N to 46°15' N
Longitude	116°45' W to 124°30' W
Highest point	Mount Hood, 11,239 feet (3,426 m)
Lowest point	Sea level along the Pacific Ocean
Largest city	Portland
Number of counties	36

Population

Population; rank (2006 estimate)	3,700,758; 27th
Density (2006 estimate)	39 persons per square mile (15 per sq km)
Population distribution (2000 census)	79% urban, 21% rural
Ethnic distribution (2005 estimate)	White persons: 90.8%*
	Asian persons: 3.4%*
	Black persons: 1.8%*
	American Indian and Alaska Native persons: 1.4%*
	Native Hawaiian and Other Pacific Islanders: 0.3%*
	Persons reporting two or more races: 2.3%
	Persons of Hispanic or Latino origin: 9.9%[†]
	White persons not Hispanic: 81.6%

Includes persons reporting only one race.
[†]*Hispanics may be of any race, so they are also included in applicable race categories.*

Weather

Record high temperature	119°F (48°C) at Prineville on July 29, 1898, and at Pendleton on August 10, 1898
Record low temperature	−54°F (−48°C) at Ukiah on February 9, 1933, and at Seneca on February 10, 1933
Average July temperature	68°F (20°C)
Average January temperature	40°F (4°C)
Average annual precipitation	37 inches (94 cm)

State flag

STATE SONG

★ ★ ★

"Oregon, My Oregon"

In 1920, a competition was held to select a state song for Oregon. The words to the winning song, "Oregon, My Oregon," were written by J. A. Buchanan, and the music is by Henry B. Murtagh. It was adopted as the state song in 1927.

Land of the empire builders, land of the golden west;
Conquered and held by free men, fairest and the best.
Onward and upward ever, forward and on and on;
Hail to thee, land of heroes, my Oregon.

Land of the rose and sunshine, land of the summer's breeze;
Laden with health and vigor, fresh from Western seas.
Blest by the blood of martyrs, land of the setting sun;
Hail to thee, land of Promise; my Oregon.

NATURAL AREAS AND HISTORIC SITES

★ ★ ★

National Park
Crater Lake National Park sits on the site of a volcano that erupted and collapsed almost 7,000 years ago. Crater Lake lies inside the collapsed volcano. Most of the year, the park is covered in snow, so snowshoers and cross-country skiers abound. In the summer, visitors can drive around the rim of the lake, hike the many trails, take boat tours, scuba dive, and fish.

National Monuments
The *Oregon Caves National Monument* features deep limestone caverns filled with stalactites, stalagmites, stone shelves and benches, and crystal clear pools.

The *Newberry National Volcanic Monument* includes 50,000 acres (20,234 ha) of lakes, lava flows, and volcanic mountains.

National Historical Parks
Lewis and Clark National Historical Park features the sites where Lewis and Clark first saw the Pacific Ocean and prepared for their return trip home.

The *Nez Perce National Historical Park* commemorates the stories and history of the Native Americans. The 38 sites of this park are found in Idaho, Oregon, Washington, and Montana.

National Memorial
Lewis and Clark and their Corps of Discovery spent the winter of 1805–1806 in a roughly built wooden fort near present-day *Fort Clatsop National Memorial*. The original fort is gone, but in 1955, Oregon citizens built a replica, using Clark's sketches.

National Historic Trails
Oregon has three different national historic trails, each with its own unique historical significance. They are the *California National Historic Trail*, the *Lewis and Clark National Historic Trail*, and the *Oregon National Historic Trail*.

National Recreation Area
Over thousands of years, the wind has swept sand into fantastic sculpted mounds at *Oregon Dunes National Recreation Area*, which visitors can explore on foot or by camel.

National Forests
Oregon has 12 national forests scattered throughout the state. Southwest Oregon's *Siskiyou National Forest*, part of the Siskiyou Mountain Range extending into northern California, has the most diverse ecology in the Pacific Northwest. *Umatilla National Forest* in northeast Oregon is located in the Blue Mountains.

SPORTS TEAMS

★ ★ ★

NCAA Teams (Division I)

Oregon State University *Beavers*
Portland State University *Vikings*
University of Oregon *Ducks*
University of Portland *Pilots*

PROFESSIONAL SPORTS TEAMS

★ ★ ★

National Basketball Association

Portland *Trail Blazers*

CULTURAL INSTITUTIONS

★ ★ ★

Libraries

The *Oregon Historical Society Library* in Portland has existed for more than 100 years. Its collections include pioneer memorabilia, Native American artwork, and various other historical collections.

Oregon State University's Valley Library in Corvallis holds millions of books, microfilm, and government documents. The main library on campus includes collections on marine biology, entomology, and mathematics.

The *Salem Public Library* has numerous events for adults and children, as well as the Discovery Room and Teen Scene area in its main branch.

Museums

Columbia River Maritime Museum celebrates Astoria's tradition as a port city.

Jordan Schnitzer Museum of Art (Eugene) has an international collection of paintings and sculpture, with an extensive display of Korean artworks.

University of Oregon Museum of Natural and Cultural History (Eugene) houses traditional fabrics, tools, weapons, and art from Africa, Asia, and New Guinea, as well as the Pacific Northwest.

The *Oregon Museum of Science and Industry* (Portland) has more than 200 hands-on exhibits.

The *Portland Art Museum* has distinguished collections of Asian, European, and Native American art, as well as works by Oregon and Washington artists.

Chinese House Railroad Museum (Echo) offers a glimpse of the railroad-building era, including a reconstructed bunkhouse where Chinese laborers lived.

Favell Museum (Klamath Falls) preserves the art and tools of Oregon's Native peoples.

Performing Arts

Oregon has one major opera company, one major symphony orchestra, two major dance companies, and one professional theater company.

Universities and Colleges

In 2006, Oregon had 26 public and 28 private institutions of higher learning.

ANNUAL EVENTS

January–March

Sled Dog Races in Chemult (January–February)

Seafood and Wine Festival in Newport (late February)

April–June

Pear Blossom Festival in Medford (mid-April)

All Northwest Barbershop Ballad Contest and Gay Nineties Festival in Forest Grove (early May)

All-Indian Rodeo in Tygh Valley (mid-May)

Rhododendron Festival in Florence (mid-May)

Cannon Beach Sandcastle Contest in Cannon Beach (May)

Fleet of Flowers Memorial Service in Depoe Bay (late May)

Oregon Shakespeare Festival in Ashland (May through October)

Strawberry Festival in Lebanon (early June)

Rose Festival and parade in Portland (June)

Bach Summer Music Festival in Eugene (late June)

July–September

Buckeroo in Molalla (early July)

Butte to Butte 10K in Eugene (early July)

Port Orford Jubilee Celebration (Fourth of July)

Rodeo in St. Paul (early July)

World Championship Timber Carnival in Albany (early July)

World Class Windsurfing in Hood River (July)

Chief Joseph Days in Joseph (late July)

Oregon Brewers Festival in Portland (late July)

Regatta in Astoria (mid-August)

State Fair in Salem (August–September)

Cycle Oregon Bike Ride in different locations (September)

Pendleton Round-Up (September)

Oktoberfest in Mount Angel (mid-September)

October–December

Lord's Acre Auction and Barbecue in Powell Butte (early November)

Kraut and Sausage Feed and Bazaar in Verboort (November)

Whale-Watching on the Oregon coast (November–December)

BIOGRAPHICAL DICTIONARY

Danny Ainge (1959–) is a Eugene-born basketball player. He played with the Boston Celtics, Portland Trail Blazers, and Phoenix Suns.

John Jacob Astor (1763–1848) was an investor who organized the Pacific Fur Company in 1810 and established Astoria in 1812.

Frederic Homer Balch (1861–1891), born in Lebanon, was a writer best known for his novel *The Bridge of the Gods*.

Carl Barks See page 83.

Pietro Belluschi See page 80.

Don Berry (1931–2001) wrote novels about life on the Oregon frontier. He was born in Minnesota and moved to Oregon as a young man.

Mel Blanc (1908–1989) was the voice behind cartoon characters such as Bugs Bunny, Porky Pig, and Barney Rubble of *The Flintstones*. He grew up in Portland.

Ann Curry

Benjamin Louis Eulalie de Bonneville (1796–1878) was a soldier who arrived in Oregon in 1832 as part of a three-year exploration of the West. He mapped much of the West and blazed part of the Oregon Trail.

Bill Bowerman (1911–1999) was a track coach at the University of Oregon who led his team to 16 winning seasons and coached many outstanding runners. He cofounded Nike, Inc.

John Callahan (1951–) is a Portland cartoonist and writer. He was paralyzed in a car accident, and his work often finds humor in disabilities and other difficulties.

Beatrice Morrow Cannady

Beatrice Morrow Cannady See page 71.

Raymond Carver (1938–1988) wrote intense stories, usually about working-class people. His collections include *Cathedral* and *Where I'm Calling From*. He was born in Clatskanie.

Marilyn Chin (1955–) is a Hong Kong–born poet who grew up in Portland. Many of her poems explore and celebrate the Asian American experience.

Beverly Cleary See page 81.

Concomly (1760?–?) was a Chinook leader who helped the Lewis and Clark expedition and the founders of Astoria.

Ann Curry (1956–) is a TV journalist who was born in Guam to a Japanese mother and French/Scots-Irish father in the U.S. Navy. She grew up in Ashland and graduated from the University of Oregon.

134

Harold Lenoir (H. L.) Davis (1896–1960), born in Yoncalla, wrote stories of frontier life in the northwestern United States. He won the 1936 Pulitzer Prize for *Honey in the Horn*.

Roscoe Lee Dixon See page 58.

David Douglas (1798–1834) was a Scottish-born botanist who explored California and Oregon in 1823–1824. The Douglas fir is named in his honor.

Abigail Scott Duniway See page 66.

Jacoby Ellsbury (1983–) is a professional baseball player who was born in Madras. He is the first person of Navajo descent to play in major league baseball.

Douglas Engelbart See page 101.

Robert Gray (1755–1806) was a fur trader and explorer who became the first American sea captain to see the mouth of the Columbia River. He named the river after his ship.

Edith Starrett Green See page 90.

Matt Groening (1954–) is a cartoonist from Portland who created *The Simpsons*. He was born in Portland.

Jacoby Ellsbury

Terri Irwin

Moses Harris (?–?) was an African American trapper and guide who led wagon trains along the Oregon Trail.

Mark Hatfield See page 93.

Hinmuuttu-yalatlat (Thunder Rolling Down Mountain) (1840?–1904) was a Nez Perce chief who tried to lead his people to Canada rather than be forced onto a reservation. White Americans called him Chief Joseph.

Herbert Hoover See page 94.

Lawson Fusao Inada (1938–) is a poet who writes about the experience and culture of Japanese Americans. He was chosen as Oregon's Poet Laureate in 2006.

Terri Irwin (1964–) is a naturalist who was born in Eugene. She is the widow of Steve Irwin and currently lives in Australia, where she owns the Australia Zoo.

Lute Jerstad (1937–1998) was among the first Americans in 1963 to reach the summit of Mount Everest. He lived in Portland.

Miranda July (1974–), born Miranda Jennifer Grossinger, is a filmmaker and short-story writer who lived in Portland for many years.

Ken Kesey (1935–2001) was a novelist who grew up in Springfield. He set his novels *One Flew over the Cuckoo's Nest* and *Sometimes a Great Notion* in Oregon.

Jon Krakauer (1954–) of Corvallis writes about the outdoors. His best-selling *Into Thin Air* (1997) tells the story of a disastrous trek up Mount Everest, the world's highest peak.

Joseph Lane (1801–1881) was a soldier and politician who served as the first governor of the Oregon Territory (1849–1850).

Jason Lee (1803–1845) was a missionary who came to the Oregon Country in 1834 and established several missions for the Indians. In 1842, he founded Willamette University, the first university west of the Mississippi.

Ursula K. Le Guin See page 82.

Barry Lopez (1945–) writes essays and books about the outdoors. His book *Arctic Dreams* won the National Book Award. He has lived in Oregon since 1968.

Larry Mahan See page 87.

Ken Kesey

Bernard Malamud (1914–1986) was a novelist and educator who wrote *The Natural*, *The Assistant*, *The Fixer*, and *A New Life*. He was born in Brooklyn, New York, and taught at Oregon State University for many years.

Edwin Markham (1852–1940), born Charles Edward Anson Markham in Oregon City, was a poet. Many of his poems, such as "The Man with the Hoe" and "Lincoln, the Man of the People," had a political slant.

Tom McCall (1913–1983) served as governor of Oregon from 1967 to 1975. He championed many laws to protect the environment.

John McLoughlin See page 42.

Joe Meek See page 47.

Wayne Morse See page 92.

Bethenia Owens-Adair See page 57.

Linus Carl Pauling (1901–1994), born in Portland, was a chemist who received the 1954 Nobel Prize in chemistry for his work on chemical bonding. He also received the 1962 Nobel Peace Prize for his work in opposing the testing of nuclear weapons in the atmosphere.

Linus Carl Pauling

Henry Lewis Pittock See page 113.

Steven Prefontaine (1951–1975) was a track star at the University of Oregon who set a series of world records.

Susan Raye (1944–), born in Eugene, is a country singer known for her 1972 hit "I've Got a Happy Heart."

John Reed (1887–1920), a native of Portland, was a journalist. His book *Ten Days That Shook the World* was an eyewitness account of the 1917 communist revolution in Russia.

Mark Rothko (1903–1970) was an abstract painter born in Latvia. He moved to Portland with his family in 1913 and later settled in New York. Many of his paintings depict large blocks of color.

Julia Ruuttila (1907–1991) was a journalist and activist who supported striking logging workers and tried to help African Americans from Vanport who lost their homes in a 1948 flood. She was from Portland.

Doc Severinsen (1927–), born in Arlington, is a jazz trumpeter who led the band on Johnny Carson's *Tonight Show* during the 1970s and 1980s.

Doc Severinsen

Mary Decker Slaney

Mary Decker Slaney (1958–) is a runner from Eugene. She broke many national and world records.

William Stafford (1914–1993) was a poet and teacher who sometimes wrote poems inspired by the natural beauty of the Northwest. His books of poetry include *Traveling Through the Dark* (1962), *The Earth* (1974), and *Who Are You Really, Wanderer?* (1993).

William Simon U'Ren See page 65.

Frances Fuller Victor (1826–1902) was a poet, writer, and historian who wrote the two-volume *History of Oregon*.

Henry Villard See page 56.

Marie Watt (1967–) is a Native American sculptor who lives and works in Portland. Most of her work explores Native American history and contemporary life.

Opal Whiteley See page 19.

Nathaniel Jarvis Wyeth (1802–1856) was a trader and explorer who built Fort William at the mouth of the Willamette River.

RESOURCES

BOOKS

Nonfiction

Griskey, Michele. *Beverly Cleary*. Hockessin, Del.: Mitchell Lane Publishers, 2006.

Harness, Cheryl. *The Tragic Tale of Narcissa Whitman and a Faithful History of the Oregon Trail*. Washington, D.C.: National Geographic, 2006.

Josephy, Alvin M. *Lewis and Clark Through Indian Eyes*. New York: Vintage, 2007.

Uschan, Michael V. *The Oregon Trail*. Milwaukee, Wis.: World Almanac Library, 2004.

Wadsworth, Ginger. *Words West: Voices of Young Pioneers*. New York: Clarion, 2003.

Whiteley, Opal. *Opal: The Journal of an Understanding Heart*. 1920. Reprint, New York: Three Rivers, 1995.

Fiction

Bunting, Eve. *The Summer of Riley*. New York: Joanna Cotler, 2001.

Carr, Mary Jane. *Children of the Covered Wagon*. Peabody, Mass.: Christian Liberty Press, 2007.

Cleary, Beverly. *The Ramona Collection*. New York: HarperTrophy, 2006.

Hermes, Patricia. *A Perfect Place*. New York: Scholastic Inc., 2002.

Thompson, Gare. *Our Journey West: The Oregon Trail Adventures of Sarah Marshall*. Washington, D.C.: National Geographic, 2003.

Van Leeuwen, Jean. *Bound for Oregon*. New York: Puffin, 1996.

Veltfort, Ruhama. *The Promised Land*. Minneapolis: Milkweed Editions, 1998.

VIDEOs

Chinese in the Frontier West: An American Story. Center for Educational Telecommunications, 2001.
Lewis and Clark: Great Journey West. National Geographic, 2002.
The Oregon Trail. Boettcher, 2002.

WEB SITES AND ORGANIZATIONS

Echoes of Oregon

arcweb.sos.state.or.us/echoes/ defaultechoes.html
This site, which covers Oregon history from 1837 to 1859 in documents and pictures, is designed for students and teachers.

Oregon Government

www.oregon.gov
Find out what the Oregon legislature is up to and get lots of other information.

Oregon Historical Society

www.ohs.org/
This site describes events and exhibits of the Oregon Historical Society and contains biographies of many Oregonians.

Oregon History Project

www.ohs.org/education/oregonhistory/
To find first-person narratives from explorers and pioneers, photos, government records, lesson plans for teachers, and interactive displays that show how Oregon has changed over time.

Oregon Trail History Library

www.endoftheoregontrail.org/histhome.html
For pictures and essays about the Corps of Discovery, the early fur traders, and the Oregon Trail.

A Place Called Oregon

www.chenowith.k12.or.us/tech/subject/ social/oregon.html
For information on Oregon's first people, mountain men, life during World War II, place-names, and much more.

Travel Oregon

www.traveloregon.com
Oregon's official tourism site offers lots of suggestions about where to visit and what to do.

INDEX

★ ★ ★

AUTHOR'S TIPS AND SOURCE NOTES

★ ★ ★

Several books on Oregon proved valuable in my research for this book. Among them are *Oregon's Promise: An Interpretive History*, by David Peterson del Mar; *The Great Northwest: A History*, by Oscar Osburn Winther; *Landscapes of Promise: The Oregon Story, 1800–1940*, by William G. Robbins; and *The Oregon Indians: Voices from Two Centuries*, edited by Stephen Dow Beckham. An extremely useful Web site from the Oregon Historical Society (www.ohs.org/education/oregonhistory/) has many firsthand accounts that bring history to life. The Web site Uniting to Understand Racism (http://oregonuniting.esiteasp.com) offers a thorough history of race issues in Oregon. I find it is most useful to read full-length histories, taking extensive notes, and then to explore Web sites to gather current information.